Theologica Germanica

Anonymous

Originally Published by Martin Luther

a lamp post book

THEOLOGICA GERMANICA
By Anonymous, Orignally Published by Martin Luther

ISBN# 1-60039-110-9

Layout and Design Copyright © 2008 by Lamp Post Inc.
Additional Content Copyright © 2008 by Lamp Post Inc.
Electronic Version Copyright © 2008 by Christian Classics Ethereal Library. All rights reserved. Ownership of this electronic version resides with the Christian Classics Ethereal Library at ccel.org.

All rights reserved. No part of this publication may be reproduced, stored in a retrieval system, or transmitted in any form or by any means (electronic, mechanical, photocopy, recording, or any other) except for brief quotations in printed reviews, without the prior permission of the publisher.

Lamp Post assumes no responsibility for any errors or inaccuracies that may appear in this book.

Requests for information should be addressed to:
LAMP PoST Inc.
www.lamppostpubs.com

"Next to the Bible and St. Augustine, no book has ever come into my hands from which I have learnt more of God and Christ, and man and all things that are."

--MARTIN LUTHER

Theologia Germanica

Which setteth forth many fair Lineaments of divine Truth,
and saith very lofty and lovely things touching a perfect life

EDITED BY DR. PEIFFER FROM THE ONLY
COMPLETE MANUSCRIPT YET KNOWN

Translated from the German by
Susanna Winkworth

With a Preface by the Rev. Charles Kingsley
Rector of Eversley, and a Letter to the Translator by the
Chevalier Bunsen, D.D., D.C.L., etc.

First published as a volume of the Golden Treasury Series in 1874.
New Edition 1893
Reprinted 1901, 1907

Scanned from the 1893 Golden Treasury Series edition
by John H. Richards (jhr@elidor.demon.co.uk), March 1995

Introductory material scanned from the 1907 reprint
by Harry Plantinga (hplantin@calvin.edu), 1996

STRONG Son of God, Immortal Love,
Whom we, that have not seen Thy face,
By faith, and faith alone embrace,
Believing where we cannot prove.

*   *   *   *   *

Thou seemest human and divine,
The highest, holiest manhood Thou;
Our wills are ours, we know not how,
Our wills are ours to make them Thine.

*   *   *   *   *

O Living Will that shalt endure,
When all that seems shall suffer shock
Rise in the spiritual Rock,
Flow through our deeds and make them pure.

*   *   *   *   *

That we may lift, from out the dust,
A voice as unto Him that hears,
A cry above the conquered years,
To one that with us works, and trust

*   *   *   *   *

With faith that comes of self-control
The truths that never can be proved,
Until we close with all we loved
find all we flow from, soul in soul.

TENNYSON

PREFACE

TO those who really hunger and thirst after righteousness; and who therefore long to know what righteousness is, that they may copy it: To those who long to be freed, not merely from the punishment of sin after they die, but from sin itself while they live on earth; and who therefore wish to know what sin is, that they may avoid it: To those who wish to be really justified by faith, by being made just persons by faith; and who cannot satisfy either their consciences or reasons by fancying that God looks on them as right, when they know themselves to be wrong, or that the God of truth will stoop to fictions (miscalled forensic) which would be considered false and unjust in any human court of law: To those who cannot help trusting that union with Christ must be something real and substantial, and not merely a metaphor, and a flower of rhetoric: To those, lastly, who cannot help seeing that the doctrine of Christ in every man, as the Indwelling Word of God, The Light who lights every one who comes into the world, is no peculiar tenet of the Quakers, but one which runs through the whole of the Old and New Testaments, and without which they would both be unintelligible, just as the same doctrine runs through the whole history of the Early Church for the first two centuries, and is the only explanation of them;

To all these this noble little book will recommend itself; and may God bless the reading of it to them, and to all others no less.

As for its orthodoxy; to "evangelical" Christians Martin Luther's own words ought to be sufficient warrant. For he has said that he owed more to this, than to any other book, saving the Bible and Saint Augustine. Those, on the other hand, to whom Luther's name does not seem a sufficient guarantee, must recollect, that the Author of this book was a knight of the Teutonic order; one who considered himself, and was considered, as far as we know, by his contemporaries, an orthodox member of the Latin Church; that his friends and disciples were principally monks exercising a great influence in the Catholic Church of their days; that one of their leaders was appointed by Pope John XXII. Nuncio and overseer of the Dominican order in Germany; and that during the hundred and seventy years which elapsed between the writing of this book and the Reformation, it incurred no ecclesiastical censure whatsoever, in generations which were but too fond of making men offenders for a word.

Not that I agree with all which is to be found in this book. It is for its noble views of righteousness and of sin that I honour it, and rejoice at seeing it published in English, now for the first time from an edition based on the perfect manuscript. But even in those points in which I should like to see it altered, I am well aware that there are strong authorities against me. The very expression, for instance, which most startles me, "*vergottet*," deified or made divine, is used, word for word, both by Saint Athanase and Saint Augustine, the former of whom has said: "He became man, that we might be made God;"[1] and the latter, "He called men Gods, as being deified by His grace, not as born of

---

1 Αὐτός ἐπηνθρώπησεν ἵνα ἡμεῖς θεοποιηθῶμεν—
Athan. *Orat. de Incarn. Verbi*, tom. I. page. 108.

His substance."[2] There are many passages, moreover, in the Epistles of the Apostles, which, if we paraphrase them at all, we can hardly paraphrase in weaker words. It seems to me safer and wiser to cling to the letter of Scripture: but God forbid that I should wish to make such a man as the Author of the *Theologia Germanica* an offender for a word!

One point more may be worthy of remark. In many obscure passages of this book, words are used, both by the Author and by the Translator, in their strict, original, and scientific meaning, as they are used in the Creeds, and not in that meaning which has of late crept into our very pulpits, under the influence of Locke's philosophy. When, for instance, it is said that God is the *Substance* of all things; this expression, in the vulgar Lockite sense of substance, would mean that God is the matter or stuff of which all things are made; which would be the grossest Pantheism: but "Substance" in the true and ancient meaning of the word, as it appears in the Athanasian Creed, signifies the very opposite; namely, that which *stands under* the appearance and the matter; that by virtue of which a thing has its form, its life, its real existence, as far as it may have any; and thus in asserting that God is the substance of all things, this book means that everything (except sin, which is no thing, but the disease and fall of a thing) is a thought of God.

So again with Eternity. It will be found in this book to mean not merely some future endless duration, but that ever-present moral world, governed by ever-living and absolutely necessary laws, in which we and all spirits are now; and in which we should be equally, whether time and space, extension and duration, and the whole material universe to which they belong, became nothing this moment, or lasted endlessly.

I think it necessary to give these cautions, because by the light of Locke's philosophy, little or nothing will be discerned in this book,

---

2 "Homines dixit Deos, ex gradia sua *deificatos*; non de substantia sua natos,"—Aug. *in Psalm xlix.* (Ed. Bened. tom. iv. page 414.)

and what little is discerned will probably be utterly misunderstood. If any man wishes to see clearly what is herein written, let him try to forget all popular modern dogmas and systems, all popular philosophies (falsely so called), and be true to the letter of his Bible, and to the instincts which the Indwelling Word of God was wont to awaken in his heart, while he was yet a little unsophisticated child; and then let him be sure that he will find in this book germs of wider and deeper wisdom than its good author ever dreamed of; and that those great spiritual laws, which the Author only applies, and that often inconsistently, to an ascetic and passively contemplative life, will hold just as good in the family, in the market, in the senate, in the study, ay, in the battlefield itself; and teach him the way to lead, in whatsoever station of life he may be placed, a truly manlike, because a truly Christlike and Godlike, life.

CHARLES KINGSLEY
Torquay, *Lent*,
1854

HISTORICAL INTRODUCTION BY THE TRANSLATOR

THE Treatise before us was discovered by Luther, who first brought it into notice by an Edition of it which he published in 1516. A Second Edition, which came out two years later, he introduced with the following Preface:—

> "We read that St. Paul, though he was of a weak and contemptible presence, yet wrote weighty and powerful letters, and he boasts of himself that his 'speech is not with enticing words of man's device,' but 'full of the riches of all knowledge and wisdom.' And if we consider the wondrous ways of God, it is clear, that He hath never chosen mighty and eloquent preachers to speak His word, but as it is written: 'Out of the mouths of babes and sucklings hast thou perfected praise,' Ps. 8:2. And again, 'For wisdom opened the mouth of the dumb, and made the tongues of them that cannot

speak eloquent,' Wisdom 10:21. Again, He blameth such as are high-minded and are offended at these simple ones. *Consilium inopis,* etc. 'Ye have made a mock at the counsel of the poor, because he putteth his trust in the Lord,' Ps. 14:6.

"This I say because I will have every one warned who readeth this little book, that he should not take offence, to his own hurt, at its bad German, or its crabbed and uncouth words. For this noble book, though it be poor and rude in words, is so much the richer and more precious in knowledge and divine wisdom. And I will say, though it be boasting of myself and 'I speak as a fool,' that next to the Bible and St. Augustine, no book hath ever come into my hands, whence I have learnt, or would wish to learn more of what God, and Christ, and man and all things are; and now I first find the truth of what certain of the learned have said in scorn of us theologians of Wittemberg, that we would be thought to put forward new things, as though there had never been men elsewhere and before our time. Yea, verily, there have been men, but God's wrath, provoked by our sins, hath not judged us worthy to see and hear them; for it is well known that for a long time past such things have not been treated of in our universities; nay, it has gone so far, that the Holy Word of God is not only laid on the shelf, but is almost mouldered away with dust and moths. Let as many as will, read this little book, and then say whether Theology is a new or an old thing among us; for this book is not new. But if they say as before, that we are but German theologians, we will not deny it. I thank God, that I have heard and found my God in the German tongue, as neither I nor they have yet found Him in the Latin, Greek, or Hebrew tongue. God grant that this book may be spread abroad, then we shall find that the German theologians are without doubt the best theologians.

(Signed, without date,)
Dr. MARTIN LUTHER,
AUGUSTINIAN of Wittemberg

These words of Luther will probably be considered to form a sufficient justification for an attempt to present the *Theologia Germanica* in an English dress. When Luther sent it forth, its effort to revive the consciousness of spiritual life was received with enthusiasm by his fellow-countrymen, in whom that life was then breaking with volcanic energy through the clods of formalism and hypocrisy, with which the Romish Church had sought to stifle its fires. No fewer than seventeen editions of the work appeared during the lifetime of Luther. Up to the present day, it has continued to be a favourite handbook of devotion in Germany, where it has passed through certainly as many as sixty Editions, and it has also been widely circulated in France and the Netherlands, by means of Latin, French, and Flemish translations.

To the question, who was the author of a book which has exerted so great an influence? no answer can be given, all the various endeavours to discover him having proved fruitless. Till within the last few years, Luther was our sole authority for the text of the work, but, about 1850, a manuscript of it was discovered at Wurtzburg, by Professor Reuss, the librarian of the University there, which has since been published verbatim by Professor Pfeiffer of Prague. This Manuscript dates from 1497; consequently it is somewhat older than Luther's time, and it also contains some passages not found in his editions. As, upon careful comparison, it seemed to the translator indisputably superior to the best modern editions based upon Luther's, it has been selected as the groundwork of the present translation, merely correcting from the former, one or two passages which appeared to contain errors of the press, or more likely of the transcriber's pen. The passages not found in Luther's edition are here enclosed between brackets.

As has been stated, the author of the *Theologia Germanica* is unknown; but it is evident from his whole cast of thought, as well as from a Preface attached to the Wurtzburg Manuscript, that he belonged to a class of men who sprang up in Southern Germany at the beginning of the fourteenth century, and who were distinguished for their earnest piety and their practical belief in the presence of the Spirit of God with all Christians, laity as well as clergy.

These men had fallen upon evil times. Their age was not indeed one of those periods in which the vigour of the nobler powers of the soul is enfeebled by the abundance of material prosperity and physical enjoyment, nor yet one of those in which they are utterly crushed out under the hoof of oppression and misery; but it was an age in which conflicting elements were wildly struggling for the mastery. The highest spiritual and temporal authorities were at deadly strife with each other and among themselves; and in their contests, there were few provinces or towns that did not repeatedly suffer the horrors of war. The desolation caused by its ravages was however speedily repaired during the intervals of peace, by the extraordinary energy which the German nation displayed in that bloom of its manhood; so that times of deep misery and great prosperity rapidly alternated with each other. But on the whole, during the first half of this century, the sense of the calamities, which were continually recurring, predominated over the recollection of the calmer years, which were barely sufficient to allow breathing time between the successive waves that threatened to overwhelm social order and happiness.

The unquestioning faith and honest enthusiasm which had prompted the Crusades, no longer burnt with the same fierce ardour, for the unhappy issue of those sacred enterprises, and the scandalous worldly ambition of the heads of the Church, had moderated its fervour and saddened the hearts of true believers. Yet the one Catholic, Christian creed still held an undivided and very real sovereignty over men's minds, and the supremacy of the Church in things spiritual was never questioned, though many were beginning to feel that it was needful for the State to have an independent authority in things temporal, and the question was warmly agitated how much of the spiritual authority resided in the Pope and how much in the bishops and doctors of the Church. But in whichever way the dispute between these rival claims might be adjusted, the reverence for the *office* of the clergy remained unimpaired. The case was very different with the reverence for their *persons,* which had fallen to a very low ebb, owing to the worldliness and immorality of their lives. This again was much encouraged by the conduct of the Popes, who, in their zeal to establish worldly dominion, made ecclesiastical appointments rather with a view to gain political adherents, or to acquire wealth by the sale of benefices, than with a regard to the fitness of the men selected, or the welfare of the people committed to their charge.

On the whole, it was an age of faith, though by no means of a blind, unreasoning taking things for granted. On the contrary, the evidences of extreme activity of mind meet us on every hand, in the monuments of its literature, architecture, and invention. A few facts strikingly illustrate the divergent tendencies of thought and public opinion. Thus we may remember, how it was currently reported that the profligate Pope Boniface VIII. was privately an unbeliever, even deriding the idea of the immortality of the soul, at the very time when he was maintaining against Philip the Fair, the right of the Pope to sit, as Christ's representative, in judgment on the living and the dead, and to take the sword of temporal power out of the hands of those who misused it.[3] Whether this

---

3   Neander's "*Kirchengeschichte,*" Band 6, S. 15, 20. This work and Schmitz's "*Johannes Tauler von Strasburg,*" are the authorities for most of the facts here mentioned.

accusation was true or not, it is a remarkable sign of the times that it should have been widely believed.

Some years later, and when the increased corruptness of the clergy, after the removal of the Papal Court to Avignon, provoked still louder complaints, we see the religious and patriotic Emperor, Louis IV., accusing John XXII. of heresy, in a public assembly held in the square of St. Peter's at Rome, and setting up another Pope "in order to please the Roman people." But though the new Pope was every way fitted, by his unblemished character and ascetic manners, to gain a hold on public esteem, we see that the Emperor could not maintain him against the legitimately elected Pope, who, from his seat at Avignon, had power to harass the Emperor so greatly with his interdicts, that the latter, finding all efforts at conciliation fruitless, would have bought peace by unconditional submission, had not the Estates of the Empire refused to yield to such humiliation. Yet we find this very Pope obliged to yield and retract his opinions on a point of dogmatic theology. He had in a certain treatise propounded the opinion that the souls of the pious would not be admitted to the immediate vision of the Deity until after the day of judgment. The King of France, in 1333, called an assembly of Prelates and theologians at his palace at Vincennes, where he invited them to discuss before him the two questions, whether the souls of departed saints would be admitted to an immediate vision of the Deity before the resurrection; and whether, if so, their vision would be of the same or of a different kind after the Judgment Day? The theological faculty having come to conclusions differing in some respects from those of the Pope, the King threatened the latter with the stake as a heretic, unless he retracted; and John XXII. issued a bull, declaring that what he had said or written, ought only to be received in so far as it agreed with the Catholic Faith, the Church and Holy Scripture. No circumstance, perhaps, offers a more remarkable spectacle to us in its contrast with the spirit of our own times. At the present moment, when the Pope could not sit for a day in safety on his temporal throne without the defence of French or

Austrian bayonets, we can scarcely conceive an Emperor of France or Austria taking upon himself to convene an assembly of Catholic theologians, and the latter pronouncing a censure on the dogmas propounded by the Head of the Church! It would be hard to say whether the Sovereigns of the present day would be more amused by the absurdity of devoting their time to such discussions, or the consciences of good Catholics more shocked at the presumption of such a verdict.

Still it must not be forgotten that the importance of religious affairs in that age must not be ascribed too exclusively to earnestness about religion itself, for the ecclesiastical interest predominated over the purely religious. The Pope and the Emperor represented the two great antagonistic powers, spiritual and temporal, the rivalry between which absorbed into itself all the political and social questions that could then be agitated. The question of allegiance to the Pope or the Emperor was like the contest between royalism and republicanism; the Ghibelline called himself a patriot, and was called by his adversary, the Guelf, a worldly man or even an infidel, while he retorted by calling the Guelf a betrayer of his country, and an enemy of national liberties.

We cannot help seeing, however, that in those days both princes and people, wicked as their lives often were, did really believe in the Christian religion, and that while much of the mythological and much of the formalistic element mingled in their zeal for outward observances, there was also much thoroughly sincere enthusiasm among them. But both the two great powers oppressed the people, which looked alternately to the one side or the other for emancipation from the particular grievances felt to be most galling at any given moment or place. In the frightful moral and physical condition of society, it was no wonder that a despair of Providence should have begun to attack some minds, which led to materialistic scepticism, while others sought for help on the path of wild speculation. The latter appears to have been the case with the Beghards or "Brothers and Sisters of the Free Spirit," who attempted to institute a reform by withdrawing the people altogether from the influence of the clergy, but whose followers after a time too often fell into the vices of the priests from whom they had separated themselves. In 1317, we find the Bishop of Ochsenstein complaining that Alsace was filled with these Beghards, who appear to have been a kind of antinomian pantheists, teaching that the Spirit is bound by no law, and annihilating the distinction between the Creator and the creature. Both in their excellences and defects they remind us of the modern "German Catholics," and of some, too, of the recent Protestant schools in Germany. There seems to have been no party of professed unbelievers, but that some individuals were such in word as well as deed, appears from what Ruysbroch of Brussels,[4] (1300-1330) says of those "who live in mortal sin, not troubling themselves about God or His grace, but thinking virtue sheer nonsense, and the spiritual life hypocrisy or delusion; and hearing with disgust all mention of God or virtue, for they are persuaded that there is no such thing as God, or Heaven, or Hell; for they acknowledge nothing but what is palpable to the senses."

The early part of the fourteenth century saw Germany divided for nine years between the rival claims of two Emperors, Frederick of Austria, supported by Pope John XXII. and a faction in Germany, and Louis of Bavaria, whose cause was espoused by a majority of the princes of the Empire, as that of the defender of the dignity and independence of the State, and the champion of reform within the Church. The death of Frederick, in 1322, left Louis the undisputed Emperor, as far as nearly all his subjects were concerned, and he would fain have purchased peace with the Pope on any reasonable terms, that he might apply himself to the internal improvement of his dominions; but John XXII. was implacable, and continued to wage against him and his adherents a deadly warfare, not closed until his successor Charles IV. submitted to all the papal demands, and to every indignity imposed upon him.

One of the most fearful consequences of the enmity between John

---

4   As quoted by Neander. *Kirchengeschichte*, B. 6, S. 769.

XXII. and Louis of Bavaria, to the unfortunate subjects of the latter, was the Interdict under which his dominions were laid in 1324, and from which some places, distinguished for their loyalty to the Emperor, were not relieved for six-and-twenty years. Louis, indeed, desired his subjects to pay no regard to the bull of excommunication, and most of the laity, especially of the larger towns, would gladly have obeyed him in spite of the Pope; but the greater part of the bishops and clergy held with their spiritual head, and thus the inhabitants of Strasburg, Nuremberg, and other cities, where the civil authorities sided with the Emperor, and the clergy with the Pope, were left year after year without any religious privileges; for public worship ceased, and all the business of life went on without the benedictions of the Church, no rite being allowed but baptism and extreme unction.

After this had lasted sixteen years, the Emperor, wishing to relieve the anguished consciences of his people, issued, in conjunction with the Princes of the Empire, a great manifesto to all Christendom, refuting the Pope's accusations against him, maintaining that he who had been legally chosen by the Electors was, in virtue thereof, the rightful Emperor, and had received his dignity from God, and proclaiming that all who denied this were guilty of high treason; that therefore none should be allowed any longer to observe the Interdict, and all who should continue to do so, whether communities or individuals, should be deprived of every civil and ecclesiastical right and privilege. This courageous edict found a response in the heart of the nation, and public opinion continually declared itself more strongly on the side of the Emperor. Yet on the whole it rather increased the general anarchy; for in many places the priests and monks were steadfast in their allegiance to the Pope, and, refusing to administer public service, were altogether banished from the towns, and the churches and convents closed. In Strasburg, for instance, where the regular clergy had long since ceased to perform religious rites, the Dominicans and Franciscans had continued to preach and perform mass; but now they too, frightened by the Edict, which placed them in direct opposition to the Pope, dared no longer to disregard the renewed sentence of excommunication hanging over them, and refusing to read mass, were expelled by the Town Council. Many of these banished clergy wandered about in great distress, with difficulty finding refuge among the scattered rural population, and the sufferings they endured proved the sincerity of their conscientious scruples. Some few, either from worldly motives, or out of pity for the people, remained at their posts. The former indeed throve by the miseries of their fellow-creatures, driving a usurious trade in the famine of spiritual consolation; for it is upon record, that in time of pestilence, the price of shrift has been as much as sixty florins!

The spectacle of such discord between the clergy and the laity was something unspeakably shocking to the Christian world in that age, and the energetic proceedings of the magistracy must have utterly staggered the faith of many. Of all the events that were stirring up men's passions and energies, none was more calculated to move their souls to the very centre, than to find themselves compelled to stand up in arms against those whom they had been wont to bow down before, and to reverence as the source of those spiritual blessings, for the sake of which they were now driven in desperation to take this awful step.

To these political and religious dissensions were added, in process of time, other miseries. After it had been preceded by earthquakes, hurricanes and famine, the Black Death broke out, spreading terror and desolation through Southern Europe. Men saw in these frightful calamities the judgments of God, but looked in vain for any to show them a way of deliverance and escape. Some believed that the last day was approaching; some, remembering an old prophecy, looked with hope for the return of the Great Emperor Frederick II. to restore justice and peace in the world, to punish the wicked clergy, and help the poor and oppressed flock to their rights. Others traversed the country in processions, scourging themselves and praying with a loud voice, in order to atone for their sins and appease God's anger, and inveighing against man's unbelief, which had called down God's wrath upon the earth; while some thought to do God service, by wreaking vengeance on the people which had slain the Lord, and thousands of wretched Jews perished in the flames kindled by frantic terror. "All things worked together to deepen the sense of the corruptness of the Church, to lead men's thoughts onwards from their physical to their spiritual wants, to awaken reflection on the judgments of God, and to fix their eyes on the indications of the future,"[5] so that John of Winterthur was probably not alone in applying to his own times what St. Paul says of the perils of the latter days.

In these chaotic times, and in the countries where the storms raged most fiercely, there were some who sought that peace which could not be found on earth, in intercourse with a higher world. Destitute of help and comfort and guidance from man, they took refuge in God, and finding that to them He had proved "a present help in time of trouble," "as the shadow of a great rock in a weary land," they tried to bring their fellow-men to believe and partake in a life raised above the troubles of this world. They desired to show them that that Eternal life and enduring peace which Christ had promised to His disciples, was, of a truth, to be found by the Way which He had pointed out,—by a living union with Him and the Father who had sent Him.

With this aim, like-minded men and women joined themselves together, that by communion of heart and mutual counsel they might strengthen each other in their common efforts to revive the spiritual life of those around them. The Association they founded was kept secret, lest through misconception of their principles, they might fall under suspicion of heresy, and the Inquisition should put a stop to their labours; but they desired to keep themselves aloof from every thing that savoured of heresy or disorder. On the contrary, they carefully observed all the precepts of the Ch9urch, and carried their obedience so far that many of their number were among the priests who were banished for

---

5   Neander, *Kircshengeschichte*, B. 6, S. 728.

obeying the Pope, when the Emperor ordered them to disregard the Interdict. They assumed the appellation of "Friends of God" *(Gottesfreunde)*, and, in the course of a few years, their associations extended along the Rhine provinces from Basle to Cologne, and eastwards through Swabia, Bavaria, and Franconia. Strasburg, Constance, Nuremberg and Nordlingen were among their chief seats. Their distinguishing doctrines were self-renunciation,—the complete giving-up of self-will to the will of God;—the continuous activity of the Spirit of God in all believers, and the intimate union possible between God and man;—the worthlessness of all religion based upon fear or the hope of reward;—and the essential equality of the laity and clergy, though, for the sake of order and discipline, the organization of the Church was necessary. They often appealed to the declaration of Christ (John 15:15), "Henceforth I call you not servants; for the servant knoweth not what his lord doeth; but I have called you friends; for all things that I have heard of my Father I have made known unto you;" and from this they probably derived their name of "Friends of God." Their mode of action was simply personal, for they made no attempt to gain political and hierarchical power, but exerted all their influence by means of preaching, writing and social intercourse. The Association counted among its members priests, monks, and laity, without distinction of rank or sex. Its leaders stood likewise in close connection with several convents, especially those of Engenthal, and Maria-Medingen near Nuremberg, presided over by the sisters Christina and Margaret Ebner, much of whose correspondence is still extant. Agnes, the widow of King Andrew of Hungary, and various knights and burghers, are also named as belonging to it.

Foremost among the leaders of this party should be mentioned the celebrated Tauler, a Dominican monk of Strasburg, who spent his life in preaching and teaching up and down the country from Strasburg to Cologne, and whose influence is to this day active among his countrymen by means of his admirable sermons, which are still widely read. At the time of the Interdict he wrote a noble appeal to the clergy not to forsake their flocks, maintaining that if the Emperor had sinned, the blame lay with him only, not with his wretched subjects, so that it was a crying shame to visit his guilt upon the innocent people, but that their unjust oppression would be recompensed to them by God hereafter. He acted up to his own principles, and when the Black Death was raging in Strasburg, where it carried off 16,000 victims, he was unwearied in his efforts to administer aid and consolation to the sick and dying.

Much of Tauler's religious fervour and light he himself attributed to the instructions of a layman, his friend. It is now known from contemporary records that this was Nicholas of Basle, a citizen of that Free town and a secret Waldensian. Little is known of his life beyond the fact that he was intimately connected with many of the heads of this party, and was resorted to by them for guidance and help; for, being under suspicion of heresy, he had to conceal all his movements from the Inquisition. He succeeded, however, in carrying on his labours and eluding his enemies, until he reached an advanced age; but at length, venturing alone and unprotected into France, he was taken, and burnt at Vienne in 1382. Another friend of Tauler's, and like him an eloquent and powerful preacher, whose sermons are still read with delight, was Henry Suso, a Dominican monk, belonging to a knightly family in Swabia.

One of the leaders of the "Friends of God," Nicholas of Strasburg, was in 1326 appointed by John XXII. nuncio, with the oversight of the Dominican order throughout Germany, and dedicated to that Pope an Essay of great learning and ability, refuting the prevalent interpretations of Scripture, which referred the coming of Antichrist and the Judgment day to the immediate future. Thus we see that the "Friends of God" were not confined to one political party, and this likewise appears from the history of another celebrated member of this sect, Henry of Nordlingen, a priest of Constance, who, like Suso, was banished for his adherence to the Pope. One of the most remarkable men of this sect was a layman and married, Rulman Merswin, belonging to a high family at Strasburg. He appears to have been led to a religious life by the influence of Tauler, who was his confessor. He is the author of several mystical works which, he says, he wrote "to do good to his fellow creatures," but he contributed perhaps still more largely to their benefit by his activity in charitable works, for he established one hospital and seems to have had the oversight of others also. He likewise gave largely to churches and convents, but is best known by having founded a house for the Knights of St. John in Strasburg. The characteristic doctrines of the "Friends of God" have already been indicated. That they should not have fallen into some exaggerations was scarcely possible, but where they have done so, it may generally be traced to the influence of the monastic life to which most of them were dedicated, and to the perplexities of their age.

The book before us was probably written somewhere about 1350, since it refers to Tauler as already well known. It was the practice of the "Friends of God" to conceal their names as much as possible when they wrote, lest a desire for fame should mingle with their endeavours to be useful. This is probably the reason why we have no indication of its authorship beyond a preface, which the Wurtzburg Manuscript possesses in common with that which was in Luther's hands, and from which it appears that the writer "was of the Teutonic order, a priest and a warden in the house of the Teutonic order in Frankfort." A translation of this Preface is prefixed to the present volume. Till the discovery of the Wurtzburg Manuscript, it was supposed that this Preface was from Luther's hand, who merely embodied in it the tradition which he had received from some source unknown to us; and hence, some, disregarding its authority, have ascribed the *Theologia Germanica* to Tauler, whose style it resembles so much that it might be taken for his work, but for the reference to him already mentioned. Since, however, the antiquity of the Preface is now proved, we must be content with the information which it affords us, unless any further discoveries among old manuscripts should throw fresh light upon the subject.

Should this attempt to introduce the writings of the "Friends of God" in England awaken an interest in them and their works, the Translator proposes to follow up the present volume with an account of Tauler and selections from his writings; believing that the study of these German theologians, who were already called old in Luther's age, would furnish the best antidote to what of mischief English readers may have derived from German theology, falsely so called.

Manchester, *February* 1854.

LETTER FROM CHEVALIER BUNSEN TO THE TRANSLATOR

77 Marina, St. Leonard's-on-Sea,

11th May 1854

MY DEAR FRIEND,

YOUR Letter and the proof-sheets of your Translation of the *Theologia Germanica*, with Kingsley's Preface and your Introduction, were delivered to me yesterday, as I was leaving Carlton Terrace to breathe once more, for a few days, the refreshing air of this quiet, lovely place. You told me, at the time, that you had been led to study Tauler and the *Theologia Germanica* by some conversations which we had on their subjects in 1851, and you now wish me to state to your readers, in a few lines, what place I conceive this school of Germanic theology to hold in the general development of Christian thought, and what appears to me to be the bearing of this work in particular upon the present dangers and prospects of Christianity, as well as upon the eternal interests of religion in the heart of every man and woman.

In complying willingly with your request, I may begin by saying that, with Luther, I rank this short treatise next to the Bible, but, unlike him, should place it before rather than after St. Augustine. That school of pious, learned, and profound men of which this book is, as it were, the popular catechism, was the Germanic counterpart of Romanic scholasticism, and more than the revival of that Latin theology which produced so many eminent thinkers, from Augustine, its father, to Thomas Aquinas, its last great genius, whose death did not take place until after the birth of Dante, who again was the contemporary of the Socrates of the Rhenish school,—Meister Eckart, the Dominican.

The theology of this school was the first protest of the Germanic mind against the Judaism and formalism of the Byzantine and mediaeval Churches,—the hollowness of science to which scholasticism had led, and the rottenness of society which a pompous hierarchy strove in vain to conceal, but had not the power nor the will to correct. Eckart and Tauler, his pupil, brought religion home from fruitless speculation, and reasonings upon imaginary or impossible suppositions, to man's own heart and to the understanding of the common people, as Socrates did the Greek philosophy. There is both a remarkable analogy and a striking contrast between the great Athenian and those Dominican friars. Socrates did full justice to the deep ethical ideas embodied in the established religion of his country and its venerated mysteries, which he far preferred to the shallow philosophy of the sophists; but he dissuaded his pupils from seeking an initiation into the mysteries, or at least from resting their convictions and hopes upon them, exhorting them to rely, not upon the oracles of Delphi, but upon the oracle in their own bosom. The "Friends of God," on the other hand, believing (like Dante) most profoundly in the truth of the Christian religion, on which the established Church of their age, notwithstanding its corruptions, was essentially founded, recommended submission to the ordinances of the church as a wholesome preparatory discipline for many minds. Like the saint of Athens, however, they spoke plain truth to the people. To their disciples, and those who came to them for instruction, they exhibited the whole depth of that real Christian philosophy, which opens to the mind after all scholastic conventionalism has been thrown away, and the soul listens to the response which Christ's Gospel and God's creation find in a sincere heart and a self-sacrificing life;—a philosophy which, considered merely as a speculation, is far more profound than any scholastic system. But, in a style that was intelligible to all, they preached that no fulfilment of rites and ceremonies, nor of so-called religious duties,—in fact, no outward works, however meritorious, can either give peace to man's conscience, nor yet give him strength to bear up against the temptations of prosperity and the trials of adversity.

In following this course they brought the people back from hollow profession and real despair, to the blessings of gospel religion, while they opened to philosophic minds a new career of thought. By teaching that man is justified by 'faith, and by faith alone, they prepared the popular intellectual element of the Reformation; by teaching that this faith has its philosophy, as fully able to carry conviction to the understanding, as faith is to give peace to the troubled conscience, they paved the way for that spiritual philosophy of the mind, of which Kant laid the foundation. But they were not controversialists, as the Reformers of the sixteenth century were driven to be by their position, and not men of science exclusively, as the masters of modern philosophy in Germany were and are. Although most of them friars, or laymen connected with the religious orders of the time, they were men of the people and men of action. They preached the saving faith to the people in churches, in hospitals, in the streets and public places. In the strength of this faith, Tauler, when he had been already for years the universal object of admiration as a theologian and preacher through all the free cities on the Rhine, from Basle to Cologne, humbled himself, and remained silent for the space of two years, after the mysterious layman had shown him the insufficiency of his scholastic learning and preaching. In the strength of this faith, he braved the Pope's Interdict, and gave the consolations of religion to the people of Strasburg, during the dreadful plague which depopulated that flourishing city. For this faith, Eckart suffered with patience slander and persecution, as formerly he had borne with meekness, honours and praise. For this faith, Nicolaus of Basle, who sat down as a humble stranger at Tauler's feet to become the instrument of his real enlightenment, died a martyr in the flames. In this sense, the "Friends of God" were, like the Apostles, men of the people and practical Christians, while as men of thought, their ideas contributed powerfully to the great efforts of the European nations in the sixteenth century.

Let me, therefore, my dear friend, lay aside all philosophical and theological terms, and state the principle of the golden book which you are just presenting to the English public, in what I consider, with Luther, the best Theological exponent, in plain Teutonic, thus:—

Sin is selfishness:

Godliness is unselfishness:

A godly life is the steadfast working out of inward freeness from self:

To become thus Godlike is the bringing back of man's first nature.

On this last point,—man's divine dignity and destiny,—Tauler speaks as strongly as our author, and almost as strongly as the Bible. Man is indeed to him God's own image. "As a sculptor," he says somewhere, with a striking range of mind for a monk of the fourteenth century, "is said to have exclaimed indignantly on seeing a rude block of marble, 'what a godlike beauty thou hidest!' thus God looks upon man in whom God's own image is hidden." "We may begin," he says in a kindred passage, "by loving God in hope of reward, we may express ourselves concerning Him in symbols *(Bilder)*, but we must throw them all away, and much more we must scorn all idea of reward, that we may love God only because He is the Supreme Good, and contemplate His eternal nature as the real substance of our own soul."

But let no one imagine that these men, although doomed to passiveness in many respects, thought a contemplative or monkish life a condition of spiritual Christianity, and not rather a danger to it. "If a man truly loves God," says Tauler, "and has no will but to do God's will, the whole force of the river Rhine may run at him and will not disturb him or break his peace; if we find outward things a danger and disturbance, it comes from our appropriating to ourselves what is God's." But Tauler, as well as our Author, uses the strongest language to express his horror of Sin, man's own creation, and their view on this subject forms their great contrast to the philosophers of the Spinozistic school. Among the Reformers, Luther stands nearest to them, with respect to the great fundamental points of theological teaching, but their intense dread of Sin as a rebellion against God, is shared both by Luther and Calvin. Among later theologians, Julius Muller, in his profound Essay on Sin, and Richard Rothe, in his great work on Christian Ethics, come nearest to them in depth of thought and ethical earnestness, and the first of these eminent writers carries out, as it appears to me, most consistently that fundamental truth of the *Theologia Germanica* that there is no sin but Selfishness, and that all Selfishness is sin.

Such appear to me to be the characteristics of our book and of Tauler. I may be allowed to add, that this small but golden Treatise has been now for almost forty years an unspeakable comfort to me and to many Christian friends (most of whom have already departed in peace), to whom I had the happiness of introducing it. May it in your admirably faithful and lucid translation become a real "book for the million" in England, a privilege which it already shares in Germany with Tauler's matchless Sermons, of which I rejoice to hear that you are making a selection for publication. May it become a blessing to many a longing Christian heart in that dear country of yours, which I am on the point of leaving, after many happy years of residence, but on which I can never look as a strange land to me, any more than I shall ever consider myself as a stranger in that home of old Teutonic liberty and energy, which I have found to be also the home of practical Christianity and of warm and faithful affection.

Bunsen

Theologica Germanica

1.

Of that which is perfect and that which is in part, and how that which is in part is done away, when that which is perfect is come.

St. Paul saith, "When that which is perfect is come, then that which is in part shall be done away."[6] Now mark what is "that which is perfect," and "that which is in part."

"That which is perfect" is a Being, who hath comprehended and included all things in Himself and His own Substance, and without whom, and beside whom, there is no true Substance, and in whom all things have their Substance. For He is the Substance of all things, and is in Himself unchangeable and immoveable, and changeth and moveth all

---

6   1 Cor. 13:10.

things else. But "that which is in part," or the Imperfect, is that which hath its source in, or springeth from the Perfect; just as a brightness or a visible appearance floweth out from the sun or a candle, and appeareth to be somewhat, this or that. And it is called a creature; and of all these "things which are in part," none is the Perfect. So also the Perfect is none of the things which are in part. The things which are in part can be apprehended, known, and expressed; but the Perfect cannot be apprehended, known, or expressed by any creature as creature. Therefore we do not give a name to the Perfect, for it is none of these. The creature as creature cannot know nor apprehend it, name nor conceive it.

"Now when that which is Perfect is come, then that which is in part shall be done away." But when doth it come? I say, when as much as may be, it is known, felt and tasted of the soul. For the lack lieth altogether in us, and not in it. In like manner the sun lighteth the whole world, and is as near to one as another, yet a blind man seeth it not; but the fault thereof lieth in the blind man, not in the sun. And like as the sun may not hide its brightness, but must give light unto the earth (for heaven indeed draweth its light and heat from another fountain), so also God, who is the highest Good, willeth not to hide Himself from any, wheresoever He findeth a devout soul, that is thoroughly purified from all creatures. For in what measure we put off the creature, in the same measure are we able to put on the Creator; neither more nor less. For if mine eye is to see anything, it must be single, or else be purified from all other things; and where heat and light enter in, cold and darkness must needs depart; it cannot be otherwise.

But one might say, "Now since the Perfect cannot be known nor apprehended of any creature, but the soul is a creature, how can it be known by the soul?" Answer: This is why we say, "by the soul as a creature." We mean it is impossible to the creature in virtue of its creature-nature and qualities, that by which it saith "I" and "myself." For in whatsoever creature the Perfect shall be known, therein creature-nature, qualities, the I, the Self and the like, must all be lost and done away. This is the meaning of that saying of St. Paul: "When that which is perf come" (that is, when it is known), "then that which is in part" (to wit, creature-nature, qualities, the I, the Self, the Mine) will be despised and counted for nought. So long as we think much of these things, cleave to them with love, joy, pleasure or desire, so long remaineth the Perfect unknown to us.

But it might further be said, "Thou sayest, beside the Perfect there is no Substance, yet sayest again that somewhat floweth out from it: now is not that which hath flowed out from it, something beside it." Answer: This is why we say, beside it, or without it, there is no true Substance. That which hath flowed forth from it, is no true Substance, and hath no Substance except in the Perfect, but is an accident, or a brightness, or a visible appearance, which is no Substance, and hath no Substance except in the fire whence the brightness flowed forth, such as the sun or a candle.

2.
Of what Sin is, and how we must not take unto ourselves any good Thing, seeing that it belongeth unto the true Good alone.

The Scripture and the Faith and the Truth say, Sin is nought else, but that the creature turneth away from the unchangeable Good and betaketh itself to the changeable; that is to say, that it turneth away from the Perfect to "that which is in part" and imperfect, and most often to itself. Now mark: when the creature claimeth for its own anything good, such as Substance, Life, Knowledge, Power, and in short whatever we should call good, as if it were that, or possessed that, or that were itself, or that proceeded from it,—as often as this cometh to pass, the creature goeth astray. What did the devil do else, or what was his going astray and his fall else, but that he claimed for himself to be also somewhat, and would have it that somewhat was his, and somewhat was due to him? This setting up of a claim and his I and Me and Mine, these were his going astray, and his fall. And thus it is to this day.

3.
How Man's Fall and going astray must be amended as Adam's Fall was.

What else did Adam do but this same thing? It is said, it was because Adam ate the apple that he was lost, or fell. I say, it was because of his claiming something for his own, and because of his I, Mine, Me, and the like. Had he eaten seven apples, and yet never claimed anything for his own, he would not have fallen: but as soon as he called something his own, he fell, and would have fallen if he had never touched an apple. Behold! I have fallen a hundred times more often and deeply, and gone a hundred times farther astray than Adam; and not all mankind could mend his fall, or bring him back from going astray. But how shall my fall be amended? It must be healed as Adam's fall was healed, and on the self-same wise. By whom, and on what wise was that healing brought to pass? Mark this: man could not without God, and God should not without man. Wherefore God took human nature or manhood upon Himself and was made man, and man was made divine. Thus the healing was brought to pass. So also must my fall be healed. I cannot do the work without God, and God may not or will not without me; for if it shall be accomplished, in me, too, God must be made man; in such sort that God must take to Himself all that is in me, within and without, so that there may be nothing in me which striveth against God or hindereth His Work. Now if God took to Himself all men that are in the world, or ever were, and were made man in them, and they were made divine in Him, and this work were not fulfilled in me, my fall and my wandering would never be amended except it were fulfilled in me also. And in this bringing back and healing, I can, or may, or shall do nothing of myself, but just simply yield to God, so that He alone may do all things in me and work, and I may suffer Him and all His work and His divine will. And because I will not do so, but I count myself to be my own, and say "I," "Mine," "Me" and the like, God is hindered, so that He cannot do His work in me alone and without hindrance; for this cause my fall and my going astray remain unhealed. Behold! this all cometh of my claiming somewhat for my own.

4.
How Man, when he claimeth any good Thing for his own, falleth, and toucheth God in His Honour.

God saith, "I will not give My glory to another."[7] This is as much as to say, that praise and honour and glory belong to none but to God only. But now, if I call any good thing my own, as if I were it, or of myself had power or did or knew anything, or as if anything were mine or of me, or belonged to me, or were due to me or the like, I take unto myself somewhat of honour and glory, and do two evil things: First, I fall and go astray as aforesaid: Secondly, I touch God in His honour and take unto myself what belongeth to God only. For all that must be called good belongeth to none but to the true eternal Goodness which is God only, and whoso taketh it unto himself, committeth unrighteousness and is against God.

---

7   Isaiah 42:8.

5.
How we are to take that Saying, that we must come to be without Will, Wisdom, Love, Desire, Knowledge, and the like.

Certain men say that we ought to be without will, wisdom, love, desire, knowledge, and the like. Hereby is not to be understood that there is to be no knowledge in man, and that God is not to be loved by him, nor desired and longed for, nor praised and honoured; for that were a great loss, and man were like the beasts and as the brutes that have no reason. But it meaneth that man's knowledge should be so clear and perfect that he should acknowledge of a truth that in himself he neither hath nor can do any good thing, and that none of his knowledge, wisdom and art, his will, love and good works do come from himself, nor are of man, nor of any creature, but that all these are of the eternal God, from whom they all proceed. As Christ Himself saith, "Without Me, ye can do nothing."[8] St. Paul saith also, "What hast thou that thou hast not received?"[9] As much as to say—nothing. "Now if thou didst receive it, why dost thou glory as if thou hadst not received it?" Again he saith, "Not that we are sufficient of ourselves to think anything as of ourselves, but our sufficiency is of God."[10] Now when a man duly perceiveth these things in himself, he and the creature fall behind, and he doth not call anything his own, and the less he taketh this knowledge unto himself, the more perfect doth it become. So also is it with the will, and love and desire, and the like. For the less we call these things our own, the more perfect and noble and Godlike do they become, and the more we think them our own, the baser and less pure and perfect do they become.

Behold on this sort must we cast all things from us, and strip our-

---

8   John 15:5.
9   1 Cor. 4:7.
10 2 Cor. 3:5.

selves of them; we must refrain from claiming anything for our own. When we do this, we shall have the best, fullest, clearest and noblest knowledge that a man can have, and also the noblest and purest love, will and desire; for then these will be all of God alone. It is much better that they should be God's than the creature's. Now that I ascribe anything good to myself, as if I were, or had done, or knew, or could perform any good thing, or that it were mine, this is all of sin and folly. For if the truth were rightly known by me, I should also know that I am not that good thing and that it is not mine, nor of me, and that I do not know it, and cannot do it, and the like. If this came to pass, I should needs cease to call anything my own.

It is better that God, or His works, should be known, as far as it be possible to us, and loved, praised and honoured, and the like, and even that man should vainly imagine he loveth or praiseth God, than that God should be altogether unpraised, unloved, unhonoured and unknown. For when the vain imagination and ignorance are turned into an understanding and knowledge of the truth, the claiming anything for our own will cease of itself. Then the man says: "Behold! I, poor fool that I was, imagined it was I, but behold! it is and was, of a truth, God!"

6.
How that which is best and noblest should also be loved above all Things by us, merely because it is the best.

A Master called Boetius saith, "It is of sin that we do not love that which is Best." He hath spoken the truth. That which is best should be the dearest of all things to us; and in our love of it, neither helpfulness nor unhelpfulness, advantage nor injury, gain nor loss, honour nor dishonour, praise nor blame, nor anything of the kind should be regarded;

but what is in truth the noblest and best of all things, should be also the dearest of all things, and that for no other cause than that it is the noblest and best.

Hereby may a man order his life within and without. His outward life: for among the creatures one is better than another, according as the Eternal Good manifesteth itself and worketh more in one than in another. Now that creature in which the Eternal Good most manifesteth itself, shineth forth, worketh, is most known and loved, is the best, and that wherein the Eternal Good is least manifested is the least good of all creatures. Therefore when we have to do with the creatures and hold converse with them, and take note of their diverse qualities, the best creatures must always be the dearest to us, and we must cleave to them, and unite ourselves to them, above all to those which we attribute to God as belonging to Him or divine, such as wisdom, truth, kindness, peace, love, justice, and the like. Hereby shall we order our outward man, and all that is contrary to these virtues we must eschew and flee from.

But if our inward man were to make a leap and spring into the Perfect, we should find and taste how that the Perfect is without measure, number or end, better and nobler than all which is imperfect and in part, and the Eternal above the temporal or perishable, and the fountain and source above all that floweth or can ever flow from it. Thus that which is imperfect and in part would become tasteless and be as nothing to us. Be assured of this: All that we have said must come to pass if we are to love that which is noblest, highest and best.

7.
Of the Eyes of the Spirit wherewith Man looketh into Eternity and into Time, and how the one is hindered of the other in its Working.

Let us remember how it is written and said that the soul of Christ had two eyes, a right and a left eye. In the beginning, when the soul of Christ was created, she fixed her right eye upon eternity and the Godhead, and remained in the full intuition and enjoyment of the divine Essence and Eternal Perfection; and continued thus unmoved and undisturbed by all the accidents and travail, suffering, torment and pain that ever befell the outward man. But with the left eye she beheld the creature and perceived all things therein, and took note of the difference between the creatures, which were better or worse, nobler or meaner; and thereafter was the outward man of Christ ordered.

Thus the inner man of Christ, according to the right eye of His soul, stood in the full exercise of His divine nature, in perfect blessedness, joy and eternal peace. But the outward man and the left eye of Christ's soul, stood with Him in perfect suffering, in all tribulation, affliction and travail; and this in such sort that the inward and right eye remained unmoved, unhindered and untouched by all the travail, suffering, grief and anguish that ever befell the outward man. It hath been said that when Christ was bound to the pillar and scourged, and when He hung upon the cross, according to the outward man, yet His inner man, or soul according to the right eye, stood in as full possession of divine joy and blessedness as it did after His ascension, or as it doth now. In like manner His outward man, or soul with the left eye, was never hindered, disturbed or troubled by the inward eye in its contemplation of the outward things that belonged to it.

Now the created soul of man hath also two eyes. The one is the power of seeing into eternity, the other of seeing into time and the creatures, of perceiving how they differ from each other as afore-said, of giving life and needful things to the body, and ordering and governing it for the best. But these two eyes of the soul of man cannot both perform their work at once; but if the soul shall see with the right eye into eternity, then the left eye must close itself and refrain from working, and be as though it were dead.

For if the left eye be fulfilling its office toward outward things; that is, holding converse with time and the creatures; then must the right eye be hindered in its working; that is, in its contemplation. Therefore whosoever will have the one must let the other go; for "no man can serve two masters."

8.
How the Soul of Man, while it is yet in the Body, may obtain a Foretaste of eternal Blessedness.

It hath been asked whether it be possible for the soul, while it is yet in the body, to reach so high as to cast a glance into eternity, and receive a foretaste of eternal life and eternal blessedness. This is commonly denied; and truly so in a sense. For it indeed cannot be so long as the soul is taking heed to the body, and the things which minister and appertain thereto, and to time and the creature, and is disturbed and troubled and distracted thereby. For if the soul shall rise to such a state, she must be quite pure, wholly stripped and bare of all images, and be entirely separate from all creatures, and above all from herself. Now many think this is not to be done and is impossible in this present time. But St. Dionysius maintains that it is possible, as we find from his words in his Epistle to Timothy, where he saith: "For the beholding of the hidden things of God, shalt thou forsake sense and the things of the flesh, and ie senses can apprehend, and all that reason of her own powers ₃ forth, and all things created and uncreated that reason is able to comprehend and know, and shalt take thy stand upon an utter abandonment of thyself, and as knowing none of the aforesaid things, and enter into union with Him who is, and who is above all existence and all knowledge." Now if he did not hold this to be possible in this present time, why should he teach it and enjoin it on us in this present time? But it behoveth you to know that a master hath said on this passage of St. Dionysius, that it is possible, and may happen to a man often, till he become so accustomed to it, as to be able to look into eternity whenever he will. For when a thing is at first very hard to a man and strange, and seemingly quite impossible, if he put all his strength and energy into it, and persevere therein, that will afterward grow quite light and easy, which he at first thought quite out of reach, seeing that it is of no use to begin any work, unless it may be brought to a good end.

And a single one of these excellent glances is better, worthier, higher and more pleasing to God, than all that the creature can perform as a creature. And as soon as a man turneth himself in spirit, and with his whole heart and mind entereth into the mind of God which is above time, all that ever he hath lost is restored in a moment. And if a man were to do thus a thousand times in a day, each time a fresh and real union would take place; and in this sweet and divine work standeth the truest and fullest union that may be in this present time. For he who hath attained thereto, asketh nothing further, for he hath found the Kingdom of Heaven and Eternal Life on earth.

9.

How it is better and more profitable for a Man that he should perceive what God will do with him, or to what end He will make Use of him, than if he knew all that God had ever wrought, or would ever work through all the Creatures; and how Blessedness lieth alone in God, and not in the Creatures, or in any Works.

We should mark and know of a very truth that all manner of virtue and goodness, and even that Eternal Good which is God Himself, can never make a man virtuous, good, or happy, so long as it is outside the soul; that is, so long as the man is holding converse with outward things through his senses and reason, and doth not withdraw into himself and learn to understand his own life, who and what he is. The like is true of sin and evil. For all manner of sin and wickedness can never make us evil, so long as it is outside of us; that is, so long as we do not commit it, or do not give consent to it.

Therefore although it be good and profitable that we should ask, and learn and know, what good and holy men have wrought and suffered, and how God hath dealt with them, and what He hath wrought in and through them, yet it were a thousand times better that we should in ourselves learn and perceive and understand, who we are, how and what our own life is, what God is and is doing in us, what He will have from us, and to what ends He will or will not make use of us. For, of a truth, thoroughly to know oneself, is above all art, for it is the highest art. If thou knowest thyself well, thou art better and more praiseworthy before God, than if thou didst not know thyself, but didst understand the course of the heavens and of all the planets and stars, also the dispositions of all mankind, also the nature of all beasts, and, in such matters, hadst all the skill of all who are in heaven and on earth. For it is said, there came a voice from heaven, saying, "Man, know thyself." Thus that proverb is still true, "Going out were never so good, but staying at home were much better."

Further, ye should learn that eternal blessedness lieth in one thing alone, and in nought else. And if ever man or the soul is to be made blessed, that one thing alone must be in the soul. Now some might ask, "But what is that one thing?" I answer, it is Goodness, or that which hath been made good; and yet neither this good nor that, which we can name, or perceive or show; but it is all and above all good things.

Moreover, it needeth not to enter into the soul, for it is there already, only it is unperceived. When we say we should come unto it, we mean that we should seek it, feel it, and taste it. And now since it is One, unity and singleness is better than manifoldness. For blessedness lieth not in much and many, but in One and oneness. In one word, blessedness lieth not in any creature, or work of the creatures, but it lieth alone in God and in His works. Therefore I must wait only on God and His work, and leave on one side all creatures with their works, and first of all myself. In like manner all the great works and wonders that God has ever wrought or shall ever work in or through the creatures, or even God Himself with all His goodness, so far as these things exist or are done outside of me, can never make me blessed, but only in so far as they exist and are done and loved, known, tasted and felt within me.

10.
How the perfect Men have no other Desire than that they may be to the Eternal Goodness what His Hand is to a Man, and how they have lost the Fear of Hell, and Hope of Heaven.

Now let us mark: Where men are enlightened with the true light, they perceive that all which they might desire or choose, is nothing to that which all creatures, as creatures, ever desired or chose or knew. Therefore they renounce all desire and choice, and commit and commend themselves and all things to the Eternal Goodness. Nevertheless, there remaineth in them a desire to go forward and get nearer to the Eternal Goodness; that is, to come to a clearer knowledge, and warmer love, and more comfortable assurance, and perfect obedience and subjection; so that every enlightened man could say: "I would fain be to the Eternal Goodness, what His own hand is to a man." And he feareth always that he is not enough so, and longeth for the salvation of all men. And such men do not call this longing their own, nor take it unto themselves, for they know well that this desire is not of man, but of the Eternal Goodness; for whatsoever is good shall no one take unto himself as his own, seeing that it belongeth to the Eternal Goodness, only.

Moreover, these men are in a state of freedom, because they have lost the fear of pain or hell, and the hope of reward or heaven, but are living in pure submission to the Eternal Goodness, in the perfect freedom of fervent love. This mind was in Christ in perfection, and is also in His followers, in some more, and in some less. But it is a sorrow and shame to think that the Eternal Goodness is ever most graciously guiding and drawing us, and we will not yield to it. What is better and nobler than true poorness in spirit? Yet when that is held up before us, we will have none of it, but are always seeking ourselves, and our own things. We like to have our mouths always filled with good things, that we may have in ourselves a lively taste of pleasure and sweetness. When this is so, we are well pleased, and think it standeth not amiss with us. But we are yet a long way off from a perfect life. For when God will draw us up to something higher, that is, to an utter loss and forsaking of our own things, spiritual and natural, and withdraweth His comfort and sweetness from us, we faint and are troubled, and can in no wise bring our minds to it; and we forget God and neglect holy exercises, and fancy we are lost for ever. This is a great error and a bad sign. For a true lover of God, loveth Him or the Eternal Goodness alike, in having and in not having, in sweetness and bitterness, in good or evil report, and the like, for he seeketh alone the honour of God, and not his own, either in spiritual or natural things. And therefore he standeth alike unshaken in all things, at all seasons. Hereby let every man prove himself, how he standeth towards God, his Creator and Lord.

11.
How a righteous Man in this present Time is brought into hell, and there cannot be comforted, and how he is taken out of Hell and carried into Heaven, and there cannot be troubled.

Christ's soul must needs descend into hell, before it ascended into heaven. So must also the soul of man. But mark ye in what manner this cometh to pass. When a man truly Perceiveth and considereth himself, who and what he is, and findeth himself utterly vile and wicked, and unworthy of all the comfort and kindness that he hath ever received from God, or from the creatures, he falleth into such a deep abasement and despising of himself, that he thinketh himself unworthy that the earth should bear him, and it seemeth to him reasonable that all creatures in heaven and earth should rise up against him and avenge their Creator on him, and should punish and torment him; and that he were unworthy even of that. And it seemeth to him that he shall be eternally lost and damned, and a footstool to all the devils in hell, and that this is right and just and all too little compared to his sins which he so often and in so many ways hath committed against God his Creator. And therefore also he will not and dare not desire any consolation or release, either from God or from any creature that is in heaven or on earth; but he is willing to be unconsoled and unreleased, and he doth not grieve over his condemnation and sufferings; for they are right and just, and not contrary to God, but according to the will of God. Therefore they are right in his eyes, and he hath nothing to say against them. Nothing grieveth him but his own guilt and wickedness; for that is not right and is contrary to God, and for that cause he is grieved and troubled in spirit.

This is what is meant by true repentance for sin. And he who in this Present time entereth into this hell, entereth afterward into the Kingdom of Heaven, and obtaineth a foretaste there of which excelleth all the delight and joy which he ever hath had or could have in this present time from temporal things. But whilst a man is thus in hell, none may console him, neither God nor the creature, as it is written, "In hell there is no redemption."[11] Of this state hath one said, "Let me perish, let me die! I live without hope; from within and from without I am condemned, let no one pray that I may be released."

Now God hath not forsaken a man in this hell, but He is laying His hand upon him, that the man may not desire nor regard anything but the Eternal Good only, and may come to know that that is so noble and passing good, that none can search out or express its bliss, consolation and joy, peace, rest and satisfaction. And then, when the man neither careth for, nor seeketh, nor desireth, anything but the Eternal Good alone, and seeketh not himself, nor his own things, but the honour of God only, he is made a partaker of all manner of joy, bliss, peace, rest and consolation, and so the man is henceforth in the Kingdom of Heaven.

---

11   The writer is probably alluding to Ps. 49:8.

This hell and this heaven are two good, safe ways for a man in this present time, and happy is he who truly findeth them.

*For this hell shall pass away,
But Heaven shall endure for aye.*

Also let a man mark, when he is in this hell, nothing may console him; and he cannot believe that he shall ever be released or comforted. But when he is in heaven, nothing can trouble him; he believeth also that none will ever be able to offend or trouble him, albeit it is indeed true, that after this hell he may be comforted and released, and after this heaven he may be troubled and left without consolation.

Again: this hell and this heaven come about a man in such sort, that he knoweth not whence they come; and whether they come to him, or depart from him, he can of himself do nothing towards it. Of these things he can neither give nor take away from himself, bring them nor banish them, but as it is written, "The wind bloweth where it listeth, and thou hearest the sound thereof," that is to say, at this time present, "but thou knowest not whence it cometh, nor whither it goeth."[12] And when a man is in one of these two states, all is right with him, and he is as safe in hell as in heaven, and so long as a man is on earth, it is possible for him to pass ofttimes from the one into the other; nay even within the space of a day and night, and all without his own doing. But when the man is in neither of these two states he holdeth converse with the creature, and wavereth hither and thither, and knoweth not what manner of man he is. Therefore he shall never forget either of them, but lay up the remembrance of them in his heart.

---

12 John 3:8.

12.
Touching that true inward Peace, which Christ left to His Disciples at the last.

Many say they have no peace nor rest, but so many crosses and trials, afflictions and sorrows, that they know not how they shall ever get through them. Now he who in truth will perceive and take note, perceiveth clearly, that true peace and rest lie not in outward things; for if it were so, the Evil Spirit also would have peace when things go according to his will, which is nowise the case; for the prophet declareth, "There is no peace, saith my God, to the wicked."[13] And therefore we must consider and see what is that peace which Christ left to His disciples at the last, when He said: "My peace I leave with you, My peace I give unto you."[14] We may perceive that in these words Christ did not mean a bodily and outward peace; for His beloved disciples, with all His friends and followers, have ever suffered, from the beginning, great affliction, persecution, nay, often martyrdom, as Christ Himself said: "In this world ye shall have tribulation."[15] But Christ meant that true, inward peace of the heart, which beginneth here, and endureth for ever hereafter. Therefore He said: "Not as the world giveth," for the world is false, and deceiveth in her gifts. She promiseth much, and performeth little. Moreover there liveth no man on earth who may always have rest and peace without troubles and crosses, with whom things always go according to his will; there is always something to be suffered here, turn which way you will. And as soon as you are quit of one assault, perhaps two come in its place. Wherefore yield thyself willingly to them, and seek only that true peace of the heart, which none can take away from thee, that thou mayest overcome all assaults.

Thus then, Christ meant that inward peace which can break through

   13   Isaiah 57:21.
   14   John 14:27.
   15   John 16:33.

all assaults and crosses of oppression, suffering, misery, humiliation and what more there may be of the like, so that a man may be joyful and patient therein, like the beloved disciples and followers of Christ. Now he who will in love give his whole diligence and might thereto, will verily come to know that true eternal peace which is God Himself, as far as it is possible to a creature; insomuch that what was bitter to him before, shall become sweet, and his heart shall remain unmoved under all changes, at all times, and after this life, he shall attain unto everlasting peace.

13.
How a Man may cast aside Images too soon.

Tauler saith: "There be some men at the present time, who take leave of types and symbols too soon, before they have drawn out all the truth and instruction contained therein." Hence they are scarcely or perhaps never able to understand the truth aright.[16] For such men will follow no one, and lean unto their own understandings, and desire to fly before they are fledged. They would fain mount up to heaven in one flight; albeit Christ did not so, for after His resurrection, He remained full forty days with His beloved disciples. No one can be made perfect in a day. A man must begin by denying himself, and willingly forsaking all things for God's sake, and must give up his own will, and all his natural inclinations, and separate and cleanse himself thoroughly from all sins and evil ways. After this, let him humbly take up the cross and follow Christ. Also let him take and receive example and instruction, reproof, counsel and teaching from devout and perfect servants of God, and not follow

> 16 Here Luther's Edition has the following passage instead of the remainder of this chapter: "Therefore we should at all times give diligent heed to the works of God and His commandments, movings, and admonitions, and not to the works or commandments or admonitions of men."

n guidance. Thus the work shall be established and come to a end. And when a man hath thus broken loose from and outleaped temporal things and creatures, he may afterwards become perfect in a life of contemplation. For he who will have the one must let the other go. There is no other way.

14.
Of three Stages by which a Man is led upwards till he attaineth true Perfection.

Now be assured that no one can be enlightened unless he be first cleansed or purified and stripped. So also, no one can be united with God unless he be first enlightened. Thus there are three stages: first, the purification; secondly, the enlightening; thirdly, the union. The purification concerneth those who are beginning or repenting, and is brought to pass in a threefold wise; by contrition and sorrow for sin, by full confession, by hearty amendment. The enlightening belongeth to such as are growing, and also taketh place in three ways: to wit, by the eschewal of sin, by the practice of virtue and good works, and by the willing endurance of all manner of temptation and trials. The union belongeth to such as are perfect, and also is brought to pass in three ways: to wit, by pureness and singleness of heart, by love, and by the contemplation of God, the Creator of all things.

15.
How all Men are dead in Adam and are made alive again in Christ, and of true Obedience and Disobedience.

All that in Adam fell and died, was raised again and made alive in Christ, and all that rose up and was made alive in Adam, fell and died in Christ. But what was that? I answer, true obedience and disobedience. But what is true obedience? I answer, that a man should so stand free, being quit of himself, that is, of his I, and Me, and Self, and Mine, and the like, that in all things, he should no more seek or regard himself, than if he did not exist, and should take as little account of himself as if he were not, and another had done all his works. Likewise he should count all the creatures for nothing. What is there then, which is, and which we may count for somewhat? I answer, nothing but that which we may call God. Behold! this is very obedience in the truth, and thus it will be in a blessed eternity. There nothing is sought nor thought of, nor loved, but the one thing only.

Hereby we may mark what disobedience is: to wit, that a man maketh some account of himself, and thinketh that he is, and knoweth, and can do somewhat, and seeketh himself and his own ends in the things around him, and hath regard to and loveth himself, and the like. Man is created for true obedience, and is bound of right to render it to God. And this obedience fell and died in Adam, and rose again and lived in Christ. Yea, Christ's human nature was so utterly bereft of Self, and apart from all creatures, as no man's ever was, and was nothing else but "a house and habitation of God." Neither of that in Him which belonged to God, nor of that which was a living human nature and a habitation of God, did He, as man, claim anything for His own. His human nature did not even take unto itself the Godhead, whose dwelling it was, nor anything that this same Godhead willed, or did or left undone in Him, nor yet anything of all that His human nature did or suffered; but in Christ's human nature there was no claiming of anything, nor seeking nor desire, saving that what was due might be rendered to the Godhead, and He did not call this very desire His own. Of this matter no more can be said, or written here, for it is unspeakable, and was never yet and never will be fully uttered; for it can neither be spoken nor written but by

Him who is and knows its ground; that is, God Himself, who can do all things well.

16.
Telleth us what is the old Man, and what is the new Man.

Again, when we read of the old man and the new man we must mark what that meaneth. The old man is Adam and disobedience, the Self, the Me, and so forth. But the new man is Christ and true obedience, a giving up and denying oneself of all temporal things, and seeking the honour of God alone in all things. And when dying and perishing and the like are spoken of, it meaneth that the old man should be destroyed, and not seek its own either in spiritual or in natural things. For where this is brought about in a true divine light, there the new man is born again. In like manner, it hath been said that man should die unto himself, that is, to earthly pleasures, consolations, joys, appetites, the I, the Self, and all that is thereof in man, to which he clingeth and on which he is yet leaning with content, and thinketh much of. Whether it be the man himself, or any other creature, whatever it be, it must depart and die, if the man is to be brought aright to another mind, according to the truth.

Thereunto doth St. Paul exhort us, saying: "Put off concerning the former conversation the old man, which is corrupt according to the deceitful lusts: . . . and that ye put on the new man, which after God is created in righteousness and true holiness."[17] Now he who liveth to himself after the old man, is called and is truly a child of Adam; and though he may give diligence to the ordering of his life, he is still the child and brother of the Evil Spirit. But he who liveth in humble obedience and in the new man which is Christ, he is, in like manner, the brother of Christ and the child of God.

17 Eph. 4:22, 24.

Behold! where the old man dieth and the new man is born, there is that second birth of which Christ saith, "Except a man be born again, he cannot enter into the kingdom of God."[18] Likewise St. Paul saith, "As in Adam all die, even so in Christ shall all be made alive."[19] That is to say, all who follow Adam in pride, in lust of the flesh, and in disobedience, are dead in soul, and never will or can be made alive but in Christ. And for this cause, so long as a man is an Adam or his child, he is without God. Christ saith, "He who is not with Me is against Me."[20] Now he who is against God, is dead before God. Whence it followeth that all Adam's children are dead before God. But he who standeth with Christ in perfect obedience, he is with God and liveth. As it hath been said already, sin lieth in the turning away of the creature from the Creator, which agreeth with what we have now said.

For he who is in disobedience is in sin, and sin can never be atoned for or healed but by returning to God, and this is brought to Pass by humble obedience. For so long as a man continueth in disobedience, his sin can never be blotted out; let him do what he will, it availeth him nothing. Let us be assured of this. For disobedience is itself sin. But when a man entereth into the obedience of the faith, all is healed, and blotted out and forgiven, and not else. Insomuch that if the Evil Spirit himself could come into true obedience, he would become an angel again, and all his sin and wickedness would be healed and blotted out and forgiven at once. And could an angel fall into disobedience, he would straightway become an evil spirit although he did nothing afresh.

If then it were possible for a man to renounce himself and all things, and to live as wholly and purely in true obedience, as Christ did in His human nature, such a man were quite without sin, and were one thing with Christ, and the same by grace which Christ was by nature. But it is said this cannot be. So also it is said: "There is none without sin." But

---

18 John 3:3.
19 1 Cor. 15:22.
20 Matt. 12:30.

be that as it may, this much is certain; that the nearer we are to perfect obedience, the less we sin, and the farther from it we are, the more we sin. In brief: whether a man be good, better, or best of all; bad, worse, or worst of all; sinful or saved before God; it all lieth in this matter of obedience. Therefore it hath been said: the more of Self and Me, the more of sin and wickedness. So likewise it hath been said: the more the Self, the I, the Me, the Mine, that is, self-seeking and selfishness, abate in a man, the more doth God's I, that is, God Himself, increase in him.

Now, if all mankind abode in true obedience, there would be no grief nor sorrow. For if it were so, all men would be at one, and none would vex or harm another; so also, none would lead a life or do any deed contrary to God's will. Whence then should grief or sorrow arise? But now alas! all men, nay the whole world lieth in disobedience! Now were a man simply and wholly obedient as Christ was, all disobedience were to him a sharp and bitter pain. But though all men were against him, they could neither shake nor trouble him, for while in this obedience a man were one with God, and God Himself were one with the man.

Behold now all disobedience is contrary to God, and nothing else. In truth, no Thing is contrary to God; no creature nor creature's work, nor anything that we can name or think of is contrary to God or displeasing to Him, but only disobedience and the disobedient man. In short, all that is, is well-pleasing and good in God's eyes, saving only the disobedient man. But he is so displeasing and hateful to God and grieveth Him so sore, that if it were possible for human nature to die a hundred deaths, God would willingly suffer them all for one disobedient man, that He might slay disobedience in him, and that obedience might be born again.

Behold! albeit no man may be so single and perfect in this obedience as Christ was, yet it is possible to every man to approach so near thereunto as to be rightly called Godlike, and "a partaker of the divine nature."[21] And the nearer a man cometh thereunto, and the more God-

---

21   2 Peter 1:4.

like and divine he becometh, the more he hateth all disobedience, sin, evil and unrighteousness, and the worse they grieve him. Disobedience and sin are the same thing, for there is no sin but disobedience, and what is done of disobedience is all sin. Therefore all we have to do is to keep ourselves from disobedience.

17.
How we are not to take unto ourselves what we have done well: but only what we have done amiss.

Behold! now it is reported there be some who vainly think and say that they are so wholly dead to self and quit of it, as to have reached and abide in a state where they suffer nothing and are moved by nothing, just as if all men were living in obedience, or as if there were no creatures. And thus they profess to continue always in an even temper of mind, so that nothing cometh amiss to them, howsoever things fall out, well or ill. Nay verily! the matter standeth not so, but as we have said. It might be thus, if all men were brought into obedience; but until then, it cannot be.

But it may be asked: Are not we to be separate from all things, and neither to take unto ourselves evil nor good? I answer, no one shall take goodness unto himself, for that belongeth to God and His goodness only; but thanks be unto the man, and everlasting reward and blessings, who is fit and ready to be a dwelling and tabernacle of the Eternal Goodness and Godhead, wherein God may exert His power, and will and work without hindrance. But if any now will excuse himself for sin, by refusing to take what is evil unto himself, and laying the guilt thereof upon the Evil Spirit, and thus make himself out to be quite pure and innocent (as our first Parents Adam and Eve did while they were yet in paradise; when each laid the guilt upon the other), he hath no right at all to do this; for it is written, "There is none without sin." Therefore I say; reproach, shame, loss, woe, and eternal damnation be to the man who is fit and ready and willing that the Evil Spirit and falsehood, lies and all untruthfulness, wickedness and other evil things should have their will and pleasure, word and work in him, and make him their house and habitation.

18.
How that the Life of Christ is the noblest and best Life that ever hath been or can be, and how a careless Life of false Freedom is the worst Life that can be.

Of a truth we ought to know and believe that there is no life so noble and good and well pleasing to God, as the life of Christ, and yet it is to nature and selfishness the bitterest life. A life of carelessness and freedom is to nature and the Self and the Me, the sweetest and pleasantest life, but it is not the best; and in some men may become the worst. But though Christ's life be the most bitter of all, yet it is to be preferred above all. Hereby shall ye mark this: There is an inward sight which hath power to perceive the One true Good, and that it is neither this nor that, but that of which St. Paul saith; "When that which is perfect is come, then that which is in part shall be done away."[22] By this he meaneth, that the Whole and Perfect excelleth all the fragments, and that all which is in part and imperfect, is as nought compared to the Perfect. Thus likewise all knowledge of the parts is swallowed up when the Whole is known; and where that Good is known, it cannot but be longed for and loved so greatly, that all other love wherewith the man hath loved himself and other things, fadeth away. And that inward sight likewise

---

22   1 Cor. 13:10.

perceiveth what is best and noblest in all things, and loveth it in the one true Good, and only for the sake of that true Good.

Behold! where there is this inward sight, the man perceiveth of a truth, that Christ's life is the best and noblest life, and therefore the most to be preferred, and he willingly accepteth and endureth it, without a question or a complaint, whether it please or offend nature or other men, whether he like or dislike it, find it sweet or bitter and the like. And therefore wherever this Perfect and true Good is known, there also the life of Christ must be led, until the death of the body. And he who vainly thinketh otherwise is deceived, and he who saith otherwise, lieth, and in what man the life of Christ is not, of him the true Good and eternal Truth will nevermore be known.

19.
How we cannot come to the true Light and Christ's Life, by much Questioning or Reading, or by high natural Skill and Reason, but by truly renouncing ourselves and all Things.

Let no one suppose, that we may attain to this true light and perfect knowledge, or life of Christ, by much questioning, or by hearsay, or by reading and study, nor yet by high skill and great learning. Yea, so long as a man taketh account of anything which is this or that, whether it be himself, or any other creature; or doeth anything, or frameth a purpose, for the sake of his own likings or desires, or opinions, or ends, he cometh not unto the life of Christ. This hath Christ Himself declared, for He saith: "If any man will come after Me, let him deny himself, and take up his cross, and follow Me."[23] "He that taketh not his cross, and followeth after Me, is not worthy of Me."[24] And if he "hate not his father

23 Matt. 16:24.
24 Matt. 10:38.

and mother, and wife, and children, and brethren and sisters, yea, and his own life also, he cannot be My disciple."[25] He meaneth it thus: "He who doth not forsake and part with everything, can never know My eternal truth, nor attain unto My life." And though this had never been declared unto us, yet the truth herself sayeth it, for it is so of a truth. But so long as a man clingeth unto the elements and fragments of this world (and above all to himself), and holdeth converse with them, and maketh great account of them, he is deceived and blinded, and perceiveth what is good no further than as it is most convenient and pleasant to himself and profitable to his own ends. These he holdeth to be the highest good and loveth above all. Thus he never cometh to the truth.

20.
How, seeing that the Life of Christ is most bitter to Nature and Self, Nature will have none of it, and chooseth a false careless Life, as is most convenient to her.

Now, since the life of Christ is every way most bitter to nature and the Self and the Me (for in the true life of Christ, the Self and the Me and nature must be forsaken and lost, and die altogether), therefore, in each of us, nature hath a horror of it, and thinketh it evil and unjust and a folly, and graspeth after such a life as shall be most comfortable and pleasant to herself, and saith, and believeth also in her blindness, that such a life is the best possible. Now, nothing is so comfortable and pleasant to nature, as a free, careless way of life, therefore she clingeth to that, and taketh enjoyment in herself and her own powers, and looketh only to her own peace and comfort and the like. And this happeneth most of all, where there are high natural gifts of reason, for that soareth upwards <u>in its own light</u> and by its own power, till at last it cometh to think itself

25 Luke 14:26.

the true Eternal Light, and giveth itself out as such, and is thus deceived in itself, and deceiveth other people along with it, who know no better, and also are thereunto inclined.

21.
How a friend of Christ willingly fulfilleth by his outward Works, such Things as must be and ought to be, and doth not concern himself with the rest.

Now, it may be asked, what is the state of a man who followeth the true Light to the utmost of his power? I answer truly, it will never be declared aright, for he who is not such a man, can neither understand nor know it, and he who is, knoweth it indeed; but he cannot utter it, for it is unspeakable. Therefore let him who would know it, give his whole diligence that he may enter therein; then will he see and find what hath never been uttered by man's lips. However, I believe that such a man hath liberty as to his outward walk and conversation, so long as they consist with what must be or ought to be; but they may not consist with what he merely willeth to be. But oftentimes a man maketh to himself many must-be's and ought-to-be's which are false. The which ye may see hereby, that when a man is moved by his pride or covetousness or other evil dispositions, to do or leave undone anything, he ofttimes saith, "It must needs be so, and ought to be so." Or if he is driven to, or held back from anything by the desire to find favour in men's eyes, or by love, friendship, enmity, or the lusts and appetites of his body, he saith, "It must needs be so, and ought to be so." Yet behold, that is utterly false. Had we no must-be's, nor ought-to-be's, but such as God and the Truth show us, and constrain us to, we should have less, forsooth, to order and do than now; for we make to ourselves much disquietude and difficulty which we might well be spared and raised above.

22.

How sometimes the Spirit of God, and sometimes also the Evil Spirit may possess a Man and have the mastery over him.

It is written that sometimes the Devil and his spirit do so enter into and possess a man, that he knoweth not what he doeth and leaveth undone, and hath no power over himself, but the Evil Spirit hath the mastery over him, and doeth and leaveth undone in, and with, and through, and by the man what he will. It is true in a sense that all the world is subject to and possessed with the Evil Spirit, that is, with lies, falsehood, and other vices and evil ways; this also cometh of the Evil Spirit, but in a different sense.

Now, a man who should be in like manner possessed by the Spirit of God, so that he should not know what he doeth or leaveth undone, and have no power over himself, but the will and Spirit of God should have the mastery over him, and work, and do, and leave undone with him and by him, what and as God would; such a man were one of those of whom St. Paul saith: "For as many as are led by the Spirit of God, they are the sons of God,"[26] and they "are not under the law, but under grace,"[27] and to whom Christ saith: "For it is not ye that speak, but the Spirit of your Father which speaketh in you."[28]

But I fear that for one who is truly possessed with the Spirit of God, there are a hundred thousand or an innumerable multitude possessed with the Evil Spirit. This is because men have more likeness to the Evil Spirit than to God. For the Self, the I, the Me and the like, all belong to the Evil Spirit, and therefore it is, that he is an Evil Spirit. Behold one or two words can utter all that hath been said by these many words: "Be

---

26 Rom. 8:14.
27 Rom. 6:14.
28 Matt. 10:20.

simply and wholly bereft of Self." But by these many words, the matter hath been more fully sifted, proved, and set forth.

Now men say, "I am in no wise prepared for this work, and therefore it cannot be wrought in me," and thus they find an excuse, so that they neither are ready nor in the way to be so. And truly there is no one to blame for this but themselves. For if a man were looking and striving after nothing but to find a preparation in all things, and diligently gave his whole mind to see how he might become prepared; verily God would well prepare him, for God giveth as much care and earnestness and love to the preparing of a man, as to the pouring in of His Spirit when the man is prepared.

Yet there be certain means thereunto, as the saying is, "To learn an art which thou knowest not, four things are needful."[29] The first and most needful of all is, a great desire and diligence and constant endeavour to learn the art. And where this is wanting, the art will never be learned. The second is, a copy or ensample by which thou mayest learn. The third is to give earnest heed to the master, and watch how he worketh, and to be obedient to him in all things, and to trust him and follow him. The fourth is to put thy own hand to the work, and practise it with all industry. But where one of these four is wanting, the art will never be learned and mastered. So likewise is it with this preparation. For he who hath the first, that is, thorough diligence and constant, persevering desire towards his end, will also seek and find all that appertaineth thereunto, or is serviceable and profitable to it. But he who hath not that earnestness and diligence, love and desire, seeketh not, and therefore findeth not, and therefore remaineth ever unprepared. And therefore he never attaineth unto that end.

---

29   See note 31.

23.

He who will submit himself to God and be obedient to Him, must be ready to bear with all Things; to wit, God, himself, and all Creatures, and must be obedient to them all whether he have to suffer or to do.

There be some who talk of other ways and preparations to this end, and say we must lie still under God's hand, and be obedient and resigned and submit to Him. This is true; for all this would be perfected in a man who should attain to the uttermost that can be reached in this present time. But if a man ought and is willing to lie still under God's hand, he must and ought also to be still under all things, whether they come from God himself, or the creatures, nothing excepted. And he who would be obedient, resigned and submissive to God, must and ought to be also resigned, obedient and submissive to all things, in a spirit of yielding, and not of resistance, and take them in silence, resting on the hidden foundations of his soul, and having a secret inward patience, that enableth him to take all chances or crosses willingly, and whatever befalleth, neither to call for nor desire any redress, or deliverance, or resistance, or revenge, but always in a loving, sincere humility to cry, "Father, forgive them, for they know not what they do!"

Behold! this were a good path to that which is Best, and a noble and blessed preparation for the farthest goal which a man may reach in this present time. This is the lovely life of Christ, for He walked in the aforesaid paths perfectly and wholly unto the end of His bodily life on earth. Therefore there is no other and better way or preparation to the joyful life of Jesus Christ, than this same course, and to exercise oneself therein, as much as may be. And of what belongeth thereunto we have already said somewhat; nay, all that we have here or elsewhere said and written, is but a way or means to that end. But what the end is, knoweth no man to declare. But let him who would know it, follow my counsel and take the right path thereunto, which is the humble life of Jesus Christ; let him strive after that with unwearied perseverance, and so, without doubt, he shall come to that end which endureth for ever. "For he that endureth to the end shall be saved."[30]

24.
How that four Things are needful before a Man can receive divine Truth and be possessed with the Spirit of God.[31]

Moreover there are yet other ways to the lovely life of Christ, besides those we have spoken of: to wit, that God and man should be wholly united, so that it can be said of a truth, that God and man are one. This cometh to Pass on this wise. Where the Truth always reigneth, so that true perfect God and true perfect man are at one, and man so giveth place to God, that God Himself is there and yet the man too, and this same unity worketh continually, and doeth and leaveth undone without any I, and Me, and Mine, and the like; behold, there is Christ, and nowhere else. Now, seeing that here there is true perfect manhood, so there is a perfect perceiving and feeling of pleasure and pain, liking and disliking, sweetness and bitterness, joy and sorrow, and all that can be perceived and felt within and without. And seeing that God is here made man, He is also able to perceive and feel love and hatred, evil and

---

30   Matt. 10:22.

31   The heading of this Chapter appears to have no relation to its contents, while it perfectly suits the latter half of Chapter xxii, which has nothing corresponding to it in the heading of that chapter. As however the heading of Chapter xxiv. is common both to the Wurtzburg MS. and Luther's editions, the translator has no option but to retain it in its present position.

good and the like. As a man who is not God, feeleth and taketh note of all that giveth him pleasure and pain, and it pierceth him to the heart, especially what offendeth him; so is it also when God and man are one, and yet God is the man; there everything is perceived and felt that is contrary to God and man. And since there man becometh nought, and God alone is everything, so is it with that which is contrary to man, and a sorrow to him. And this must hold true of God so long as a bodily and substantial life endureth.

Furthermore, mark ye, that the one Being in whom God and man are united, standeth free of himself and of all things, and whatever is in him is there for God's sake and not for man's, or the creature's. For it is the property of God to be without this and that, and without Self and Me, and without equal or fellow; but it is the nature and property of the creature to seek itself and its own things, and this and that, here and there; and in all that it doeth and leaveth undone its desire is to its own advantage and profit. Now where a creature or a man forsaketh and cometh out of himself and his own things, there God entereth in with His own, that is, with Himself.

25.
Of two evil Fruits that do spring up from the Seed of the Evil Spirit, and are two Sisters who love to dwell together. The one is called spiritual Pride and Highmindedness, the other is false, lawless Freedom.

Now, after that a man hath walked in all the ways that lead him unto the truth, and exercised himself therein, not sparing his labour; now, as often and as long as he dreameth that his work is altogether finished, and he is by this time quite dead to the world, and come out from Self and given up to God alone, behold! the Devil cometh and soweth his seed in the man's heart. From this seed spring two fruits; the one is spiritual fulness or pride, the other is false, lawless freedom. These are two sisters who love to be together. Now, it beginneth on this wise: the Devil puffeth up the man, till he thinketh himself to have climbed the topmost pinnacle, and to have come so near to heaven, that he no longer needeth Scripture, nor teaching, nor this nor that, but is altogether raised above any need. Whereupon there ariseth a false peace and satisfaction with himself, and then it followeth that he saith or thinketh: "Yea, now I am above all other men, and know and understand more than any one in the world; therefore it is certainly just and reasonable that I should be the lord and commander of all creatures, and that all creatures, and especially all men, should serve me and be subject unto me." And then he seeketh and desireth the same, and taketh it gladly from all creatures, especially men, and thinketh himself well worthy of all this, and that it is his due, and looketh on men as if they were the beasts of the field, and thinketh himself worthy of all that ministereth to his body and life and nature, in profit, or joy, or pleasure, or even pastime and amusement, and he seeketh and taketh it wherever he findeth opportunity. And whatever is done or can be done for him, seemeth him all too little and too poor, for he thinketh himself worthy of still more and greater honour than can be rendered to him. And of all the men who serve him and are subject to him, even if they be downright thieves and murderers, he saith nevertheless, that they have faithful, noble hearts, and have great love and faithfulness to the truth and to poor men. And such men are praised by him, and he seeketh them and followeth after them wherever they be. But he who doth not order himself according to the will of these high-minded men, nor is subject unto them, is not sought after by them, nay, more likely blamed and spoken ill of, even though he were as holy as St. Peter himself. And seeing that this proud and puffed-up spirit thinketh that she needeth neither Scripture, nor instruction, nor anything of the kind, therefore she giveth no heed to the admonitions, order, laws and precepts of the holy Christian Church, nor to the Sacraments, but mocketh at them and at all men who walk according to these ordinances and hold them in reverence. Hereby we may plainly see that those two sisters dwell together.

Moreover since this sheer pride thinketh to know and understand more than all men besides, therefore she chooseth to prate more than all other men, and would fain have her opinions and speeches to be alone regarded and listened to, and counteth all that others think and say to be wrong, and holdeth it in derision as a folly.

26.
Touching Poorness of Spirit and true Humility and whereby we may discern the true and lawful free Men whom the Truth hath made free.

But it is quite otherwise where there is poorness of spirit, and true humility; and it is so because it is found and known of a truth that a man, of himself and his own power, is nothing, hath nothing, can do and is capable of nothing but only infirmity and evil. Hence followeth that the man findeth himself altogether unworthy of all that hath been or ever will be done for him, by God or the creatures, and that he is a debtor to God and also to all the creatures in God's stead, both to bear with, and to labour for, and to serve them. And therefore he doth not in any wise stand up for his own rights, but from the humility of his heart he saith, "It is just and reasonable that God and all creatures should be against me, and have a right over me, and to me, and that I should not be against any one, nor have a right to anything." Hence it followeth that the man doth not and will not crave or beg for anything, either from God or the creatures, beyond mere needful things, and for those only with shamefacedness, as a favour and not as a right. And he will not minister unto or gratify his body or any of his natural desires, beyond what is needful, nor allow that any should help or serve him except in case of necessity, and then always in trembling; for he hath no right to anything and therefore he thinketh himself unworthy of anything. So likewise all his own discourse, ways, words and works seem to this man a thing of nought and a folly. Therefore he speaketh little, and doth not take upon himself to admonish or rebuke any, unless he be constrained thereto by love or faithfulness towards God, and even then he doth it in fear, and so little as may be.

Moreover, when a man hath this poor and humble spirit, he cometh to see and understand aright, how that all men are bent upon themselves, and inclined to evil and sin, and that on this account it is needful and profitable that there be order, customs, law and precepts, to the end that the blindness and foolishness of men may be corrected, and that vice and wickedness may be kept under, and constrained to seemliness. For without ordinances, men would be much more mischievous and ungovernable than dogs and cattle. And few have come to the knowledge of the truth but what have begun with holy practices and ordinances, and exercised themselves therein so long as they knew nothing more nor better.

Therefore one who is poor in spirit and of a humble mind doth not despise or make light of law, order, precepts and holy customs, nor yet of those who observe and cleave wholly to them, but with loving pity and gentle sorrow, crieth: "Almighty Father, Thou Eternal Truth, I make my lament unto Thee, and it grieveth Thy Spirit too, that through man's blindness, infirmity, and sin, that is made needful and must be, which in deed and truth were neither needful nor right." For those who are perfect are under no law.

So order, laws, precepts and the like are merely an admonition to men who understand nothing better and know and perceive not wherefore all law and order is ordained. And the perfect accept the law along with such ignorant men as understand and know nothing better, and practise it with them, to the intent that they may be restrained thereby, and kept from evil ways, or if it be possible, brought to something higher.

Behold! all that we have said of poverty and humility is so of a truth, and we have the proof and witness thereof in the pure life of Christ, and in His words. For He both practised and fulfilled every work of true humility and all other virtues, as shineth forth in His holy life, and He saith also expressly: "Learn of Me; for I am meek and lowly of heart: and ye shall find rest unto your souls."[32] Moreover He did not despise and set at nought the law and the commandments, nor yet the men who are under the law. He saith: "I am not come to destroy the law or the prophets, but to fulfil." But he saith further, that to keep them is not enough, we must press forward to what is higher and better, as is indeed true. He saith: "Except your righteousness shall exceed the righteousness of the Scribes and Pharisees, ye shall in no case enter into the kingdom of Heaven."[33] For the law forbiddeth evil works, but Christ condemneth also evil thoughts; the law alloweth us to take vengeance on our enemies, but Christ commandeth us to love them. The law forbiddeth not the good things of this world, but He counselleth us to despise them. And He hath set His seal upon all He said, with His own holy life; for He taught nothing that He did not fulfil in work, and He kept the law and was subject unto it to the end of His mortal life. Likewise St. Paul saith: "Christ was made under the law, to redeem them that were under the law."[34] That is, that He might bring them to something higher and nearer to Himself. He said again, "The Son of man came not to be ministered unto, but to minister."[35]

In a word: in Christ's life and words and works, we find nothing but true, pure humility and poverty such as we have set forth. And therefore where God dwelleth in a man, and the man is a true follower of Christ,

---

32 Matt. xi. 29.
33 Matt. 5:20.
34 Galat. 4:4.
35 Matt. 20:28.

it will be, and must be, and ought to be the same. But where there is pride, and a haughty spirit, and a light careless mind, Christ is not, nor any true follower of His.

Christ said: "My soul is troubled, even unto death." He meaneth His bodily death. That is to say: from the time that He was born of Mary, until His death on the cross, He had not one joyful day, but only trouble, sorrow and contradiction. Therefore it is just and reasonable that His servants should be even as their Master. Christ saith also: "Blessed are the poor in spirit" (that is, those who are truly humble), "for theirs is the kingdom of Heaven." And thus we find it of a truth, where God is made man. For in Christ and in all His true followers, there must needs be thorough humility and poorness of spirit, a lowly retiring disposition, and a heart laden with a secret sorrow and mourning, so long as this mortal life lasteth. And he who dreameth otherwise is deceived, and deceiveth others with him as aforesaid. Therefore nature and Self always avoid this life, and cling to a life of false freedom and ease, as we have said.

Behold! now cometh an Adam or an Evil Spirit, wishing to justify himself and make excuse, and saith: "Thou wilt almost have it that Christ was bereft of self and the like, yet He spake often of Himself, and glorified Himself in this and that." Answer: when a man in whom the truth worketh, hath and ought to have a will towards anything, his will and endeavour and works are for no end, but that the truth may be seen and manifested; and this will was in Christ, and to this end, words and works were needful. And what Christ did because it was the most profitable and best means thereunto, He no more took unto Himself than anything else that happened. Dost thou say now: "Then there was a Wherefore in Christ"? I answer, if thou wert to ask the sun, "Why shinest thou?" he would say: "I must shine, and cannot do otherwise, for it is my nature and property; but this my property, and the light I give, is not of myself, and I do not call it mine." So likewise is it with God and Christ and all who are godly and belong unto God. In them is no willing, nor working nor desiring but has for its end, goodness as goodness, for the sake of goodness, and they have no other Wherefore than this.

27.
How we are to take Christ's Words when He bade forsake all Things; and wherein the Union with the Divine Will standeth.

Now, according to what hath been said, ye must observe that when we say, as Christ also saith, that we ought to resign and forsake all things, this is not to be taken in the sense that a man is neither to do nor to purpose anything; for a man must always have something to do and to order so long as he liveth. But we are to understand by it that the union with God standeth not in any man's powers, in his working or abstaining, perceiving or knowing, nor in that of all the creatures taken together.

Now what is this union? It is that we should be of a truth purely, simply, and wholly at one with the One Eternal Will of God, or altogether without will, so that the created will should flow out into the Eternal Will, and be swallowed up and lost therein, so that the Eternal Will alone should do and leave undone in us. Now mark what may help or further us towards this end. Behold, neither exercises, nor words, nor works, nor any creature nor creature's work can do this. In this wise therefore must we renounce and forsake all things, that we must not imagine or suppose that any words, works, or exercises, any skill or cunning or any created thing can help or serve us thereto. Therefore we must suffer these things to be what they are, and enter into the union with God. Yet outward things must be, and we must do and refrain so far as is necessary, especially we must sleep and wake, walk and stand still, speak and be silent and much more of the like. These must go on so long as we live.

28.
How, after a Union with the Divine Will, the inward Man standeth immoveable, the while the outward Man is moved hither and thither.

Now, when this union truly cometh to pass and becometh established, the inward man standeth henceforward immoveable in this union; and God suffereth the outward man to be moved hither and thither, from this to that, of such things as are necessary and right. So that the outward man saith in sincerity "I have no will to be or not to be, to live or die, to know or not to know, to do or to leave undone and the like; but I am ready for all that is to be, or ought to be, and obedient thereunto, whether I have to do or to suffer." And thus the outward man hath no Wherefore or purpose, but only to do his part to further the Eternal Will. For it is perceived of a truth, that the inward man shall stand immoveable, and that it is needful for the outward man to be moved. And if the inward man have any Wherefore in the actions of the outward man, he saith only that such things must be and ought to be, as are ordained by the Eternal Will. And where God Himself dwelleth in the man, it is thus; as we plainly see in Christ. Moreover, where there is this union, which is the offspring of a Divine light and dwelleth in its beams, there is no spiritual pride or irreverent spirit, but boundless humility, and a lowly broken heart; also an honest blameless walk, justice, peace, content, and all that is of virtue must needs be there. Where they are not, there is no right union, as we have said. For just as neither this thing nor that can bring about or further this union, so there is nothing which hath power to frustrate or hinder it, save the man himself with his self-will, that doeth him this great wrong. Of this be well assured.

29.
How a Man may not attain so high before Death as not to be moved or touched by outward Things.

There be some who affirm, that a man, while in this present time, may and ought to be above being touched by outward things, and in all respects as Christ was after His resurrection. This they try to prove and establish by Christ's words: "I go before you into Galilee there; shall ye see Me."[36] And again, "A spirit hath not flesh and bones, as ye see Me have."[37] These sayings they interpret thus: "As ye have seen Me, and been followers of Me, in My mortal body and life, so also it behoveth you to see Me and follow Me, as I go before you into Galilee; that is to say, into a state in which nothing hath power to move or grieve the soul; on which state ye shall enter, and live and continue therein, before that ye have suffered and gone through your bodily death. And as ye see Me having flesh and bones, and not liable to suffer, so shall ye likewise, while yet in the body and having your mortal nature, cease to feel outward things, were it even the death of the body."

Now, I answer, in the first place, to this affirmation, that Christ did not mean that a man should or could attain unto this state, unless he have first gone through and suffered all that Christ did. Now, Christ did not attain thereunto, before He had passed through and suffered His natural death, and what things appertain thereto. Therefore no man can or ought to come to it so long as he is mortal and liable to suffer. For if such a state were the noblest and best, and if it were possible and right to attain to it, as aforesaid, in this present time, then it would have been attained by Christ; for the life of Christ is the best and noblest, the worthiest and loveliest in God's sight that ever was or will be. Therefore if it was not and could not be so with Christ, it will never be so with any

---

36 Matt. 26:32, and 28:7-10.
37 Luke 24:39.

man. Therefore though some may imagine and say that such a life is the best and noblest life, yet it is not so.

30.
On what wise we may come to be beyond and above all Custom, Order, Law, Precepts and the like.

Some say further, that we can and ought to get beyond all virtue, all custom and order, all law, precepts and seemliness, so that all these should be laid aside, thrown off and set at nought. Herein there is some truth, and some falsehood. Behold and mark: Christ was greater than His own life, and above all virtue, custom, ordinances and the like, and so also is the Evil Spirit above them, but with a difference. For Christ was and is above them on this wise, that His words, and works, and ways, His doings and refrainings, His speech and silence, His sufferings, and whatsoever happened to Him, were not forced upon Him, neither did He need them, neither were they of any profit to Himself. It was and is the same with all manner of virtue, order, laws, decency, and the like; for all that may be reached by them is already in Christ to perfection. In this sense, that saying of St. Paul is true and receiveth its fulfilment, "As many as are led by the Spirit of God, they are the sons of God," "and are not under the law, but under grace."[38] That meaneth, man need not teach them what they are to do or abstain from; for their Master, that is, the Spirit of God, shall verily teach them what is needful for them to know. Likewise they do not need that men should give them precepts, or command them to do right and not to do wrong, and the like; for the same admirable Master who teacheth them what is good or not good, what is higher and lower, and in short leadeth them into all truth, He reigneth also within them, and biddeth them to hold fast that which is

---

38 Rom. 8:14, and 6:14.

good, and to let the rest go, and to Him they give ear. Behold! in this sense they need not to wait upon any law, either to teach or to command them. In another sense also they need no law; namely, in order to seek or win something thereby or get any advantage for themselves. For whatever help toward eternal life, or furtherance in the way everlasting, they might obtain from the aid, or counsel, or words, or works of any creature, they possess already beforehand. Behold! in this sense also it is true, that we may rise above all law and virtue, and also above the works and knowledge and powers of any creature.

31.
How we are not to cast off the Life of Christ, but practise it diligently, and walk in it until Death.

But that other thing which they affirm, how that we ought to throw off and cast aside the life of Christ, and all laws and commandments, customs and order and the like, and pay no heed to them, but despise and make light of them, is altogether false and a lie. Now some may say; "Since neither Christ nor others can ever gain anything, either by a Christian life, or by all these exercises and ordinances, and the like, nor turn them to any account, seeing that they possess already all that can be had through them, what cause is there why they should not henceforth eschew them altogether? Must they still retain and practise them?"

Behold, ye must look narrowly into this matter. There are two kinds of Light; the one is true and the other is false. The true light is that Eternal Light which is God; or else it is a created light, but yet divine, which is called grace. And these are both the true Light. So is the false light Nature or of Nature. But why is the first true, and the second false? This we can better perceive than say or write. To God, as Godhead, appertain neither will, nor knowledge, nor manifestation, nor anything that we can name, or say, or conceive. But to God as God,[39] it belongeth to express Himself, and know and love Himself, and to reveal Himself to Himself; and all this without any creature. And all this resteth in God as a substance but not as a working, so long as there is no creature. And out of this expressing and revealing of Himself unto Himself, ariseth the distinction of Persons. But when God as God is made man, or where God dwelleth in a godly man, or one who is "made a partaker of the divine nature," in such a man somewhat appertaineth unto God which is His own, and belongeth to Him only and not to the creature. And without the creature, this would lie in His own Self as a Substance or well-spring, but would not be manifested or wrought out into deeds. Now God will have it to be exercised and clothed in a form, for it is there only to be wrought out and executed. What else is it for? Shall it lie idle? What then would it profit? As good were it that it had never been; nay better, for what is of no use existeth in vain, and that is abhorred by God and Nature. However God will have it wrought out, and this cannot come to pass (which it ought to do) without the creature. Nay, if there ought not to be, and were not this and that—works, and a world full of real things, and the like, —what were God Himself, and what had He to do, and whose God would He be? Here we must turn and stop, or we might follow this matter and grope along until we knew not where we were, nor how we should find our way out again.

---

39 This is, as a Person—"God" being used here as a proper name.—Tr.

32.

How God is a true, simple, perfect Good, and how He is a Light and a Reason and all Virtues, and how what is highest and best, that is, God, ought to be most loved by us.

In short, I would have you to understand, that God (in so far as He is good) is goodness as goodness, and not this or that good. But here mark one thing. Behold! what is sometimes here and sometimes there is not everywhere, and above all things and places; so also, what is to-day, or to-morrow, is not always, at all times, and above all time; and what is some thing, this or that, is not all things and above all things. Now behold, if God were some thing, this or that, He would not be all in all, and above all, as He is; and so also, He would not be true Perfection. Therefore God is, and yet He is neither this nor that which the creature, as creature, can perceive, name, conceive or express. Therefore if God (in so far as He is good) were this or that good, He would not be all good, and therefore He would not be the One Perfect Good, which He is. Now God is also a Light and a Reason,[40] the property of which is to give light and shine, and take knowledge; and inasmuch as God is Light and Reason, He must give light and perceive. And all this giving and perceiving of light existeth in God without the creature; not as a work fulfilled, but as a substance or well-spring. But for it to flow out into a work, something really done and accomplished,[41] there must be creatures through whom this can come to pass. Look ye: where this Reason and Light is at work in a creature, it perceiveth and knoweth and teacheth what itself is; how that it is good in itself and neither this thing nor that thing. This Light and Reason knoweth and teacheth men, that it is a true, simple,

---

40 Cognition is the word which comes nearest to the original *Erkenntniss*, but would not harmonise with the style of the translation.

41 Or, be realised.

perfect Good, which is neither this nor that special good, but comprehendeth every kind of good.

Now, having declared that this Light teacheth the One Good, what doth it teach concerning it? Give heed to this. Behold! even as God is the one Good and Light and Reason, so is He also Will and Love and Justice and Truth, and in short all virtues. But all these are in God one Substance, and none of them can be put in exercise and wrought out into deeds without the creature, for in God, without the creature, they are only as a Substance or well-spring, not as a work. But where the One, who is yet all these, layeth hold of a creature, and taketh possession of it, and directeth and maketh use of it, so that He may perceive in it somewhat of His own, behold, in so far as He is Will and Love, He is taught of Himself, seeing that He is also Light and Reason, and He willeth nothing but that One thing which He is.

Behold! in such a creature, there is no longer anything willed or loved but that which is good, because it is good, and for no other reason than that it is good, not because it is this or that, or pleaseth or displeaseth such a one, is pleasant or painful, bitter or sweet, or what not. All this is not asked about nor looked at. And such a creature doth nothing for its own sake, or in its own name, for it hath quitted all Self, and Me, and Mine, and We and Ours, and the like, and these are departed. It no longer saith, "I love myself, or this or that, or what not." And if you were to ask Love, "What lovest thou?" she would answer, "I love Goodness." "Wherefore?" "Because it is good, and for the sake of Goodness." So it is good and just and right to deem that if there were ought better than God, that must be loved better than God. And thus God loveth not Himself as Himself, but as Goodness. And if there were, and He knew, ought better than God, He would love that and not Himself. Thus the Self and the Me are wholly sundered from God, and belong to Him only in so far as they are necessary for Him to be a Person.

Behold! all that we have said must indeed come to pass in a Godlike man, or one who is truly "made a partaker of the divine nature"; for else he would not be truly such.

33.
How when a Man is made truly Godlike, his Love is pure and unmixed, and he loveth all Creatures, and doth his best for them.

Hence it followeth, that in a truly Godlike man, his love is pure and unmixed, and full of kindness, insomuch that he cannot but love in sincerity all men and things, and wish well, and do good to them, and rejoice in their welfare. Yea, let them do what they will to such a man, do him wrong or kindness, bear him love or hatred or the like, yea, if one could kill such a man a hundred times over, and he always came to life again, he could not but love the very man who had so often slain him, although he had been treated so unjustly, and wickedly, and cruelly by him, and could not but wish well, and do well to him, and show him the very greatest kindness in his power, if the other would but only receive and take it at his hands. The proof and witness whereof may be seen in Christ; for He said to Judas, when he betrayed Him: "Friend, wherefore art thou come?" Just as if He had said: "Thou hatest Me, and art Mine enemy, yet I love thee and am thy friend. Thou desirest and rejoicest in My affliction, and dost the worst thou canst unto Me; yet I desire and wish thee all good, and would fain give it thee, and do it for thee, if thou wouldst but take and receive it." As though God in human nature were saying: "I am pure, simple Goodness, and therefore I cannot will, or desire, or rejoice in, or do or give anything but goodness. If I am to reward thee for thy evil and wickedness, I must do it with goodness, for I am and have nothing else." Hence therefore God, in a man who is "made partaker of His nature," desireth and taketh no revenge for all the wrong that is or can be done unto Him. This we see in Christ, when He said: "Father, forgive them, for they know not what they do."

Likewise it is God's property that He doth not constrain any by force to do or not to do anything, but He alloweth every man to do and leave undone according to his will, whether it be good or bad, and resisteth none. This too we see in Christ, who would not resist or defend Himself when His enemies laid hands on Him. And when Peter would have defended Him, He said unto Peter: "Put up thy sword into the sheath: the cup which My Father hath given Me, shall I not drink it?" Neither may a man who is made a partaker of the divine nature, oppress or grieve any one. That is, it never entereth into his thoughts, or intents, or wishes, to cause pain or distress to any, either by deed or neglect, by speech or silence.

34.
How that if a Man will attain to that which is best, he must forswear his own Will; and he who helpeth a Man to his own Will helpeth him to the worst Thing he can.

Some may say: "Now since God willeth and desireth and doeth the best that may be to every one, He ought so to help each man and order things for him, that they should fall out according to his will and fulfil his desires, so that one might be a Pope, another a Bishop, and so forth." Be assured, he who helpeth a man to his own will, helpeth him to the worst that he can. For the more a man followeth after his own self-will, and self-will groweth in him, the farther off is he from God, the true Good, for nothing burneth in hell but self-will. Therefore it hath been said, "Put off thine own will, and there will be no hell." Now God is very willing to help a man and bring him to that which is best in itself, and is of all things the best for man. But to this end, all self-will must depart, as we have said. And God would fain give man His help and counsel thereunto, for so long as a man is seeking his own good, he doth not seek what is best for him, and will never find it. For a man's highest good would be and truly is, that he should not seek himself nor his own things, nor be his own end in any respect, either in things spiritual or things natural, but should seek only the praise and glory of God and His holy will. This doth God teach and admonish us. Let him therefore who wisheth that God should help him to what is best, and best for him, give diligent heed to God's counsels and teachings, and obey His commandments; thus, and not else, will he have, and hath already, God's help. Now God teacheth and admonisheth man to forsake himself and all things, and to follow Him only. "For he who loveth his soul,"[42] that is himself, and will guard it and keep it, "he shall lose it"; that is, he who seeketh himself and his own advantage in all things, in so doing loseth his soul. "But he who hateth his soul for My sake shall keep it unto life eternal"; that is, he who forsaketh himself and his own things, and giveth up his own will, and fulfilleth God's will, his soul will be kept and preserved unto Life Eternal.

---

42 Mark 8:35. Our authorised version uses the word "life" in this verse, but as that would not quite bring out the force of the original, I have ventured to use the same word for ψυχη here, by which it is translated in the two succeeding verses. Except in this and another passage, where, in quoting John 3:8, πνευμα is translated, as in Luther's version, *Spirit* instead of *Wind*, our authorised version has been always ahered to.—Tr.

35.

How there is deep and true Humility and Poorness of Spirit in a Man who is "made a Partaker of the Divine Nature."

Moreover, in a man who is "made a partaker of the divine nature," there is a thorough and deep humility, and where this is not, the man hath not been "made a partaker of the divine nature." So Christ taught in words and fulfilled in works. And this humility springeth up in the man, because in the true Light he seeth (as it also really is) that Substance, Life, Perceiving, Knowledge, Power, and what is thereof, do all belong to the True Good, and not to the creature; but that the creature of itself is nothing and hath nothing, and that when it turneth itself aside from the True Good in will or in works, nothing is left to it but pure evil. And therefore it is true to the very letter, that the creature, as creature, hath no worthiness in itself, and no right to anything, and no claim over any one, either over God or over the creature, and that it ought to give itself up to God and submit to Him because this is just. And this is the chiefest and most weighty matter.

Now, if we ought to be, and desire to be, obedient and submit unto God, we must also submit to what we receive at the hands of any of His creatures, or our submission is all false. From this latter article floweth true humility, as indeed it doth also from the former.[43] And unless this verily ought to be, and were wholly agreeable to God's justice, Christ would not have taught it in words, and fulfilled it in His life. And herein there is a veritable manifestation of God; and it is so of a truth, that of God's truth and justice this creature shall be subject to God and all creatures, and no thing or person shall be subject or obedient to her. God and all the creatures have a right over her and to her, but she hath a right to nothing: she is a debtor to all, and nothing is owing to her, so

---

43 Namely, God's having a right to our obedience.

that she shall be ready to bear all things from others, and also if needs be to do all things for others. And out of this groweth that poorness of spirit of which Christ said: "Blessed are the poor in spirit" (that is to say, the truly humble), "for theirs is the Kingdom of Heaven." All this hath Christ taught in words and fulfilled with His life.

36.
How nothing is contrary to God but Sin only; and what Sin is in Kind and Act.

Further ye shall mark: when it is said that such a thing or such a deed is contrary to God, or that such a thing is hateful to God and grieveth His Spirit, ye must know that no creature is contrary to God, or hateful or grievous unto Him, in so far as it is, liveth, knoweth, hath power to do, or produce ought, and so forth, for all this is not contrary to God. That an evil spirit, or a man is, liveth, and the like, is altogether good and of God; for God is the Being of all that are, and the Life of all that live, and the Wisdom of all the wise; for all things have their being more truly in God than in themselves, and also all their powers, knowledge, life, and the rest; for if it were not so, God would not be all good; And thus all creatures are good. Now what is good is agreeable to God, and He will have it. Therefore it cannot be contrary to Him.

But what then is there which is contrary to God and hateful to Him? Nothing but Sin. But what is Sin? Mark this: Sin is nothing else than that the creature willeth otherwise than God willeth, and contrary to Him. Each of us may see this in himself; for he who willeth otherwise than I, or whose will is contrary to mine, is my foe; but he who willeth the same as I, is my friend, and I love him. It is even so with God: and that is sin, and is contrary to God, and hateful and grievous to Him. And he who willeth, speaketh, or is silent, doeth or leaveth undone, otherwise than as I will, is contrary to me, and an offence unto me. So it is also with God: when a man willeth otherwise than God, or contrary to God, whatever he doeth or leaveth undone, in short all that proceedeth from him, is contrary to God and is sin. And whatsoever Will willeth otherwise than God, is against God's will. As Christ said: "He who is not with Me is against me." Hereby may each man see plainly whether or not he be without sin, and whether or not he be committing sin, and what sin is, and how sin ought to be atoned for, and wherewith it may be healed. And this contradiction to God's will is what we call, and is, disobedience. And therefore Adam, the I, the Self, Self-will, Sin, or the Old Man, the turning aside or departing from God, do all mean one and the same thing.

37.
How in God, as God, there can neither be Grief, Sorrow, Displeasure, nor the like, but how it is otherwise in a Man who is "made a Partaker of the Divine Nature."

In God, as God, neither sorrow nor grief nor displeasure can have place, and yet God is grieved on account of men's sins. Now since grief cannot befall God without the creature, this cometh to pass where He is made man, or when He dwelleth in a Godlike man. And there, behold, sin is so hateful to God, and grieveth Him so sore, that He would willingly suffer agony and death, if one man's sins might be thereby washed out. And if He were asked whether He would rather live and that sin should remain, or die and destroy sin by His death, He would answer that He would a thousand times rather die. For to God one man's sin is more hateful, and grieveth Him worse than His own agony and death. Now if one man's sin grieveth God so sore, what must the sins of all men do? Hereby ye may consider, how greatly man grieveth God with his sins.

And therefore where God is made man, or when He dwelleth in a truly Godlike man, nothing is complained of but sin, and nothing else is hateful; for all that is, and is done, without sin, is as God will have it, and is His. But the mourning and sorrow of a truly Godlike man on account of sin, must and ought to last until death, should he live till the Day of Judgment, or for ever. From this cause arose that hidden anguish of Christ, of which none can tell or knoweth ought save Himself alone, and therefore is it called a mystery.

Moreover, this is an attribute of God, which He will have, and is well pleased to see in a man; and it is indeed God's own, for it belongeth not unto the man, he cannot make sin to be so hateful to himself. And where God findeth this grief for sin, He loveth and esteemeth it more than ought else; because it is, of all things, the bitterest and saddest that man can endure.

All that is here written touching this divine attribute, which God will have man to possess, that it may be brought into exercise in a living soul, is taught us by that true Light, which also teacheth the man in whom this Godlike sorrow worketh, not to take it unto himself, any more than if he were not there. For such a man feeleth in himself that he hath not made it to spring up in his heart, and that it is none of his, but belongeth to God alone.

38.
How we are to put on the Life of Christ from Love, and not for the sake of Reward, and how we must never grow careless concerning it, or cast it off.

Now, wherever a man hath been made a partaker of the divine nature, in him is fulfilled the best and noblest life, and the worthiest in God's eyes, that hath been or can be. And of that eternal love which loveth Goodness as Goodness and for the sake of Goodness, a true, noble, Christ-like life is so greatly beloved, that it will never be forsaken or cast off. Where a man hath tasted this life, it is impossible for him ever to part with it, were he to live until the Judgment Day. And though he must die a thousand deaths, and though all the sufferings that ever befell all creatures could be heaped upon him, he would rather undergo them all, than fall away from this excellent life; and if he could exchange it for an angel's life, he would not.

This is our answer to the question, "If a man, by putting on Christ's life, can get nothing more than he hath already, and serve no end, what good will it do him?" This life is not chosen in order to serve any end, or to get anything by it, but for love of its nobleness, and because God loveth and esteemeth it so greatly. And whoever saith that he hath had enough of it, and may now lay it aside, hath never tasted nor known it; for he who hath truly felt or tasted it, can never give it up again. And he who hath put on the life of Christ with the intent to win or deserve ought thereby, hath taken it up as an hireling and not for love, and is altogether without it. For he who doth not take it up for love, hath none of it at all; he may dream indeed that he hath put it on, but he is deceived. Christ did not lead such a life as His for the sake of reward, but out of love; and love maketh such a life light and taketh away all its hardships, so that it becometh sweet and is gladly endured. But to him who hath not put it on from love, but hath done so, as he dreameth, for the sake of reward, it is utterly bitter and a weariness, and he would fain be quit of it. And it is a sure token of an hireling that he wisheth his work were at an end. But he who truly loveth it, is not offended at its toil or suffering, nor the length of time it lasteth. Therefore it is written, "To Serve God and live to Him, is easy to him who doeth it." Truly is so to him who doth it for love, but it is hard and wearisome to him who doth it for hire. It is the same with all virtue and good works, and likewise with order, laws, obedience to precepts, and the like. But God rejoiceth more over one man who truly loveth, than over a thousand hirelings.

39.
How God will have Order, Custom, Measure, and the like in the Creature, seeing that He cannot have them without the Creature, and of four sorts of Men who are concerned with this Order, Law, and Custom.

It is said, and truly, God is above and without custom, measure, and order, and yet giveth to all things their custom, order, measure, fitness, and the like. The which is to be thus understood. God will have all these to be, and they cannot have a being in Himself without the creature, for in God, apart from the creature, there is neither order nor disorder, custom nor chance, and so forth; therefore He will have things so that these shall be, and shall be put in exercise. For wherever there is word, work, or change, these must be either according to order, custom, measure and fitness, or according to unfitness and disorder. Now fitness and order are better and nobler than their contraries.

But ye must mark: There are four sorts of men who are concerned with order, laws, and customs. Some keep them neither for God's sake, nor to serve their own ends, but from constraint: these have as little to do with them as may be, and find them a burden and heavy yoke. The second sort obey for the sake of reward: these are men who know nothing beside, or better than, laws and precepts, and imagine that by keeping them they may obtain the kingdom of Heaven and Eternal Life, and not otherwise; and him who practiseth many ordinances they think to be holy, and him who omitteth any tittle of them they think to be lost. Such men are very much in earnest and give great diligence to the work, and yet they find it a weariness. The third sort are wicked, false-hearted men, who dream and declare that they are perfect and need no ordinances, and make a mock of them.

The fourth are those who are enlightened with the True Light, who do not practise these things for reward, for they neither look nor desire to get anything thereby, but all that they do is from love alone. And these are not so anxious and eager to accomplish much and with all speed as the second sort, but rather seek to do things in peace and good leisure; and if some not weighty matter be neglected, they do not therefore think themselves lost, for they know very well that order and fitness are better than disorder, and therefore they choose to walk orderly, yet know at the same time that their salvation hangeth not thereon. Therefore they are not in so great anxiety as the others. These men are judged and blamed by both the other parties, for the hirelings say that they neglect their duties and accuse them of being unrighteous, and the like; and the others (that is, the Free Spirits[44]) hold them in derision, and say that they cleave unto weak and beggarly elements, and the like. But these enlightened men keep the middle path, which is also the best; for a lover of God is better and dearer to Him than a hundred thousand hirelings. It is the same with all their doings.

Furthermore, ye must mark, that to receive God's commands and His counsel and all His teaching, is the privilege of the inward man, after that he is united with God. And where there is such a union, the outward man is surely taught and ordered by the inward man, so that no outward commandment or teaching is needed. But the commandments and laws of men belong to the outer man, and are needful for those men who know nothing better, for else they would not know what to do and what to refrain from, and would become like unto the dogs or other beasts.

---

44 This is evidently an allusion to the "Brethren of the Free Spirit," mentioned in the Historical Introduction.

40.

A good Account of the False Light and its Kind.

Now I have said that there is a False Light; but I must tell you more particularly what it is, and what belongeth thereunto. Behold, all that is contrary to the True Light belongeth unto the False. To the True Light it belongeth of necessity, that it seeketh not to deceive, nor consenteth that any should be wronged or deceived, neither can it be deceived. But the false is deceived and a delusion, and deceiveth others along with itself. For God deceiveth no man, nor willeth that any should be deceived, and so it is with His True Light. Now mark, the True Light is God or divine, but the False Light is Nature or natural. Now it belongeth to God, that He is neither this nor that, neither willeth nor desireth, nor seeketh anything in the man whom He hath made a partaker of the divine nature, save Goodness as Goodness, and for the sake of Goodness. This is the token of the True Light. But to the Creature and Nature it belongeth to be somewhat, this or that, and to intend and seek something, this or that, and not simply what is good without any Wherefore. And as God and the True Light are without all self-will, selfishness, and self-seeking, so do the I, the Me, the Mine, and the like, belong unto the natural and false Light; for in all things it seeketh itself and its own ends, rather than Goodness for the sake of Goodness. This is its property, and the property of nature or the carnal man in each of us.

Now mark how it first cometh to be deceived. It doth not desire nor choose Goodness as Goodness, and for the sake of Goodness, but desireth and chooseth itself and its own ends, rather than the Highest Good; and this is an error, and is the first deception.

Secondly, it dreameth itself to be that which it is not, for it dreameth itself to be God, and is truly nothing but nature. And because it imagineth itself to be God, it taketh to itself what belongeth to God; and not that which is God's, when He is made man, or dwelleth in a Godlike man, but that which is God's, and belongeth unto Him, as He is in eternity, without the creature. For, as it is said, God needeth nothing, is free, not bound to work, apart by Himself, above all things, and so forth (which is all true); and God is unchangeable, not to be moved by anything, and is without conscience, and what He doeth that is well done; "So will I be," saith the False Light, "for the more like God one is, the better one is, and therefore I will be like God and will be God, and will sit and go and stand at His right hand": as Lucifer the Evil Spirit also said.[45] Now God in Eternity is without contradiction, suffering and grief, and nothing can hurt or vex Him of all that is or befalleth. But with God, when He is made Man, it is otherwise.

In a word: all that can be deceived is deceived by this False Light. Now since all is deceived by this False Light that can be deceived, and all that is creature and nature, and all that is not God nor of God, may be deceived, and since this False Light itself is nature, it is possible for it to be deceived. And therefore it becometh and is deceived by itself, in that it riseth and climbeth to such a height that it dreameth itself to be above nature, and fancieth it to be impossible for nature or any creature to get so high, and therefore it cometh to imagine itself God. And hence it taketh unto itself all that belongeth unto God, and specially what is His as He is in Eternity, and not as He is made Man. Therefore it thinketh and declareth itself to be above all works, words, customs, laws and order, and above that life which Christ led in the body which He possessed in His holy human nature. So likewise it professeth to remain unmoved by any of the creature's works; whether they be good or evil, against God or not, is all alike to it; and it keepeth itself apart from all things, like God in Eternity, and all that belongeth to God and to no creature it taketh unto itself, and vainly dreameth that this belongeth unto it; and deemeth itself well worthy of all this, and that it is just and right that all creatures should serve it, and do it homage. And thus no contradiction, suffering or grief is left unto it; indeed nothing but a

---

45   Isaiah 14:13, 14.

mere bodily and carnal perceiving: this must remain until the death of the body, and what suffering may accrue therefrom. Furthermore, this False Light imagineth, and saith, that it has got beyond Christ's life in the flesh, and that outward things have lost all power to touch it or give it pain, as it was with Christ after His resurrection, together with many other strange and false conceits which arise and grow up from these.

And now since this False Light is nature, it possesseth the property of nature, which is to intend and seek itself and its own in all things, and what may be most expedient, easy and pleasant to nature and itself. And because it is deceived, it imagineth and proclaimeth it to be best that each should seek and do what is best for himself. It refuseth also to take knowledge of any Good but its own, that which it vainly fancieth to be Good. And if one speak to it of the One, true, everlasting Good, which is neither this nor that, it knoweth nothing thereof, and thinketh scorn of it. And this is not unreasonable, for nature as nature cannot attain thereunto. Now this False Light is merely nature, and therefore it cannot attain thereunto.

Further, this False Light saith that it hath got above conscience and the sense of sin, and that whatever it doeth is right, Yea, it was said by such a false Free Spirit, who was in this error, that if he had killed ten men he should have as little sense of guilt as if he had killed a dog. Briefly: this false and deceived Light fleeth all that is harsh and contrary to nature, for this belongeth to it, seeing that it is nature. And seeing also that it is so utterly deceived as to dream that it is God, it were ready to swear by all that is holy, that it knoweth truly what is best, and that both in belief and practice it hath reached the very summit. For this cause it cannot be converted or guided into the right path, even as it is with the Evil Spirit.

Mark further: in so far as this Light imagineth itself to be God and taketh His attributes unto itself, it is Lucifer, the Evil Spirit; but in so far as it setteth at nought the life of Christ, and other things belonging to the True Light, which have been taught and fulfilled by Christ, it is Antichrist, for it teacheth contrary to Christ. And as this Light is deceived by its own cunning and discernment, so all that is not God, or of God, is deceived by it, that is, all men who are not enlightened by the True Light and its love. For all who are enlightened by the True Light can never more be deceived, but whoso hath it not and chooseth to walk by the False Light, he is deceived.

This cometh herefrom, that all men in whom the True Light is not, are bent upon themselves, and think much of themselves, and seek and propose their own ends in all things, and whatever is most pleasant and convenient to themselves they hold to be best. And whoso declareth the same to be best, and helpeth and teacheth them to attain it, him they follow after, and maintain to be the best and wisest of teachers. Now the False Light teacheth them this very doctrine, and showeth them all the means to come by their desire; therefore all those follow after it, who know not the True Light. And thus they are together deceived.

It is said of Antichrist, that when he cometh, he who hath not the seal of God in his forehead, followeth after him, but as many as have the seal follow not after him. This agreeth with what hath been said. It is indeed true, that it is good for a man that he should desire, or come by his own good. But this cannot come to pass so long as a man is seeking, or purposing his own good; for if he is to find and come by his own highest good, he must lose it that he may find it. As Christ said: "He who loveth his life shall lose it." That is; he shall forsake and die to the desires of the flesh, and shall not obey his own will nor the lusts of the body, but obey the commands of God and those who are in authority over him, and not seek his own, either in spiritual or natural things, but only the praise and glory of God in all things. For he who thus loseth his life shall find it again in Eternal Life. That is: all the goodness, help, comfort, and joy which are in the creature, in heaven or on earth, a true lover of God findeth comprehended in God Himself; yea, unspeakably more, and as much nobler and more perfect as God the Creator is better, nobler, and more perfect than His creature. But by these excellences in the creature the False Light is deceived, and seeketh nothing but itself and its own in all things. Therefore it cometh never to the right way.

Further, this False Light saith, that we should be without conscience or sense of sin, and that it is a weakness and folly to have anything to do with them: and this it will prove by saying that Christ was without conscience or sense of sin. We may answer and say: Satan is also without them, and is none the better for that. Mark what a sense of sin is. It is that we perceive how man has turned away from God in his will (this is what we call sin), and that this is man's fault, not God's, for God is guiltless of sin. Now, who is there that knoweth himself to be free from sin save Christ alone? Scarcely will any other affirm this. Now he who is without sense of sin is either Christ or the Evil Spirit.

Briefly: where this True Light is, there is a true, just life such as God loveth and esteemeth. And if the man's life is not perfect as Christ's was, yet it is framed and builded after His, and his life is loved, together with all that agreeth with decency, order, and all other virtues, and all Self-will, I, Mine, Me, and the like, is lost; nothing is purposed or sought but Goodness, for the sake of Goodness, and as Goodness. But where that False Light is, there men become heedless of Christ's life and all virtue, and seek and intend whatever is convenient and pleasant to nature. From this ariseth a false, licentious freedom, so that men grow regardless and careless of everything. For the True Light is God's seed, and therefore it bringeth forth the fruits of God. And so likewise the False Light is the seed of the Devil; and where that is sown, the fruits of the Devil spring up—nay, the very Devil himself. This ye may understand by giving heed to what hath been said.

41.

Now that he is to be called, and is truly, a Partaker of the Divine Nature, who is illuminated with the Divine Light, and inflamed with Eternal Love, and how Light and Knowledge are worth nothing without Love.

Some may ask, "What is it to be a 'partaker of the divine nature,' or a Godlike man?" Answer: he who is imbued with or illuminated by the Eternal or divine Light, and inflamed or consumed with Eternal or divine love, he is a Godlike man and a partaker of the divine nature; and of the nature of this True Light we have said somewhat already.

But ye must know that this Light or knowledge is worth nothing without Love. This ye may see if ye call to mind, that though a man may know very well what is virtue or wickedness, yet if he doth not love virtue, he is not virtuous, for he obeyeth vice. But if he loveth virtue he followeth after it, and his love maketh him an enemy to wickedness, so that he will not do or practise it, and hateth it also in other men; and he loveth virtue so that he would not leave a virtue unpractised even if he might, and this for no reward, but simply for the love of virtue. And to him virtue is its own reward, and he is content therewith, and would take no treasure or riches in exchange for it. Such an one is already a virtuous man, or he is in the way to be so. And he who is a truly virtuous man would not cease to be so, to gain the whole world, yea, he would rather die a miserable death.

It is the same with justice. Many a man knoweth full well what is just or unjust, and yet neither is nor ever will become a just man. For he loveth not justice, and therefore he worketh wickedness and injustice. If he loved justice, he would not do an unjust thing; for he would feel such hatred and indignation towards injustice wherever he saw it, that he would do or suffer anything that injustice might be put an end to, and men might become just. And he would rather die than do an injustice, and all this for nothing but the love of justice. And to him, justice is her own reward, and rewardeth him with herself; and so there liveth a just man, and he would rather die a thousand times over than live as an unjust man. It is the same with truth: a man may know full well what is true or a lie, but if he loveth not the truth he is not a true man; but if he loveth, it is with truth even as with justice. Of justice speaketh Isaiah in the fifth chapter: "Woe unto them that call evil good, and good evil; that put darkness for light, and light for darkness; that put bitter for sweet, and sweet for bitter!"

Thus may we perceive that knowledge and light profit nothing without Love. We see this in the Evil Spirit; he perceiveth and knoweth good and evil, right and wrong, and the like; but since he hath no love for the good that he seeth, he becometh not good, as he would if he had any love for the truth and other virtues which he seeth. It is indeed true that Love must be guided and taught of Knowledge, but if Knowledge be not followed by love, it will avail nothing. It is the same with God and divine things. Let a man know much about God and divine things, nay, dream that he seeth and understandeth what God Himself is, if he have not Love, he will never become like unto God, or a "partaker of the divine nature." But if there be true Love along with his knowledge, he cannot but cleave to God, and forsake all that is not God or of Him, and hate it and fight against it, and find it a cross and a sorrow.

And this Love so maketh a man one with God, that he can nevermore be separated from Him.

42.
A Question: whether we can know God and not love Him, and how there are two kinds of Light and Love—a true and a false.

Here is an honest question; namely, it hath been said that he who knoweth God and loveth Him not, will never be saved by his knowledge; the which sounds as if we might know God and not love Him. Yet we have said elsewhere, that where God is known, He is also loved, and whosoever knoweth God must love Him. How may these things agree? Here ye must mark one thing. We have spoken of two Lights—a True and a False. So also there are two kinds of Love, a True and a False. And each kind of Love is taught or guided by its own kind of Light or Reason. Now, the True Light maketh True Love, and the False Light maketh False Love; for whatever Light deemeth to be best, she delivereth unto Love as the best, and biddeth her love it, and Love obeyeth, and fulfilleth her commands.

Now, as we have said, the False Light is natural, and is Nature herself. Therefore every property belongeth unto it which belongeth unto nature, such as the Me, the Mine, the Self, and the like; and therefore it must needs be deceived in itself and be false; for no I, Me, or Mine, ever came to the True Light or Knowledge undeceived, save once only; to wit, in God made Man. And if we are to come to the knowledge of the simple Truth, all these must depart and perish. And in particular it belongeth to the natural Light that it would fain know or learn much, if it were possible, and hath great pleasure, delight and glorying in its discernment and knowledge; and therefore it is always longing to know more and more, and never cometh to rest and satisfaction, and the more it learneth and knoweth, the more doth it delight and glory therein. And when it hath come so high, that it thinketh to know all things and to be above all things, it standeth on its highest pinnacle of delight and glory, and then it holdeth Knowledge to be the best and noblest of all things, and therefore it teacheth Love to love knowledge and discernment as the best and most excellent of all things. Behold, then knowledge and discernment come to be more loved than that which is discerned, for the false natural Light loveth its knowledge and powers, which are itself, more than that which is known. And were it possible that this false natural Light should understand the simple Truth, as it is in God and in truth, it still would not lose its own property, that is, it would not depart from itself and its own things. Behold, in this sense there is knowledge without the love of that which is or may be known.

Also this Light riseth and climbeth so high that it vainly thinketh that it knoweth God and the pure, simple Truth, and thus it loveth itself in Him. And it is true that God can be known only by God. Wherefore as this Light vainly thinketh to understand God, it imagineth itself to be God, and giveth itself out to be God, and wisheth to be accounted so, and thinketh itself to be above all things, and well worthy of all things, and that it hath a right to all things, and hath got beyond all things, such as commandments, laws, and virtue, and even beyond Christ and a Christian life, and setteth all these at nought, for it doth not set up to be Christ, but the Eternal God. And this is because Christ's life is distasteful and burdensome to nature, therefore she will have nothing to do with it; but to be God in eternity and not man, or to be Christ as He was after His resurrection, is all easy, and pleasant, and comfortable to nature, and so she holdeth it to be best. Behold, with this false and deluded Love, something may be known without being loved, for the seeing and knowing is more loved than that which is known. Further, there is a kind of learning which is called knowledge; to wit, when, through hearsay, or reading, or great acquaintance with Scripture, some fancy themselves to know much, and call it knowledge, and say, "I know this or that." And if you ask, "How dost thou know it?" they answer, "I have read it in the Scriptures," and the like. Behold, this they call understanding, and knowing. Yet this is not knowledge, but belief, and many things are known and loved and seen only with this sort of perceiving and knowing.

There is also yet another kind of Love, which is especially false, to wit, when something is loved for the sake of a reward, as when justice is loved not for the sake of justice, but to obtain something thereby, and so on. And where a creature loveth other creatures for the sake of something that they have, or loveth God, for the sake of something of her own, it is all false Love; and this Love belongeth properly to nature, for nature as nature can feel and know no other love than this; for if ye look narrowly into it, nature as nature loveth nothing beside herself. On this wise something may be seen to be good and not loved.

But true Love is taught and guided by the true Light and Reason, and this true, eternal and divine Light teacheth Love to love nothing but the One true and Perfect Good, and that simply for its own sake, and not for the sake of a reward, or in the hope of obtaining anything, but simply for the Love of Goodness, because it is good and hath a right to be loved. And all that is thus seen by the help of the True Light must also be loved of the True Love. Now that Perfect Good, which we call God, cannot be perceived but by the True Light; therefore He must be loved wherever He is seen or made known.

43.
Whereby we may know a Man who is made a partaker of the divine Nature, and what belongeth unto him; and further, what is the token of a False Light, and a False Free-Thinker.

Further mark ye; that when the True Love and True Light are in a man, the Perfect Good is known and loved for itself and as itself; and yet not so that it loveth itself of itself and as itself, but the one True and Perfect

Good can and will love nothing else, in so far as it is in itself, save the one, true Goodness. Now if this is itself, it must love itself, yet not as itself nor as of itself, but in this wise: that the One true Good loveth the One Perfect Goodness, and the One Perfect Goodness is loved of the One, true and Perfect Good. And in this sense that saying is true, that "God loveth not Himself as Himself." For if there were ought better than God, God would love that, and not Himself. For in this True Light and True Love there neither is nor can remain any I, Me, Mine, Thou, Thine, and the like, but that Light perceiveth and knoweth that there is a Good which is all Good and above all Good, and that all good things are of one substance in the One Good, and that without that One, there is no good thing. And therefore, where this Light is, the man's end and aim is not this or that, Me or Thee, or the like, but only the One, who is neither I nor Thou, this nor that, but is above all I and Thou, this and that; and in Him all Goodness is loved as One Good, according to that saying: "All in One as One, and One in All as All, and One and all Good, is loved through the One in One, and for the sake of the One, for the love that man hath to the One."

Behold, in such a man must all thought of Self, all self-seeking, self-will, and what cometh thereof, be utterly lost and surrendered and given over to God, except in so far as they are necessary to make up a person. And whatever cometh to pass in a man who is truly Godlike, whether he do or suffer, all is done in this Light and this Love, and from the same, through the same, unto the same again. And in his heart there is a content and a quietness, so that he doth not desire to know more or less, to have, to live, to die, to be, or not to be, or anything of the kind; these become all one and alike to him, and he complaineth of nothing but of sin only. And what sin is, we have said already, namely, to desire or will anything otherwise than the One Perfect Good and the One Eternal Will, and apart from and contrary to them, or to wish to have a will of one's own. And what is done of sin, such as lies, fraud, injustice, treachery, and all iniquity, in short, all that we call sin, cometh hence, that man hath another will than God and the True Good; for were there no will but the One Will, no sin could ever be committed. Therefore we may well say that all self-will is sin, and there is no sin but what springeth therefrom. And this is the only thing which a truly Godlike man complaineth of; but to him, this is such a sore pain and grief, that he would die a hundred deaths in agony and shame, rather than endure it; and this his grief must last until death, and where it is not, there be sure that the man is not truly Godlike, or a partaker of the divine nature.

Now, seeing that in this Light and Love, all Good is loved in One and as One, and the One in all things, and in all things as One and as All, therefore all those things must be loved that rightly are of good report; such as virtue, order, seemliness, justice, truth, and the like; and all that belongeth to God is the true Good and is His own, is loved and praised; and all that is without this Good, and contrary to it, is a sorrow and a pain, and is hated as sin, for it is of a truth sin. And he who liveth in the true Light and true Love, hath the best, noblest, and worthiest life that ever was or will be, and therefore it cannot but be loved and praised above any other life. This life was and is in Christ to perfection, else He were not the Christ.

And the love wherewith the man loveth this noble life and all goodness, maketh, that all which he is called upon to do, or suffer, or pass through, and which must needs be, he doeth or endureth willingly and worthily, however hard it may be to nature. Therefore saith Christ: "My yoke is easy, and My burden is light."[46] This cometh of the love which loveth this admirable life. This we may see in the beloved Apostles and Martyrs; they suffered willingly and gladly all that was done unto them, and never asked of God that their suffering and tortures might be made shorter, or lighter or fewer, but only that they might remain steadfast and endure to the end. Of a truth all that is the fruit of divine Love in a truly Godlike man is so simple, plain, and straightforward, that he can never properly give an account of it by writing or by speech, but only

---

46 Matt. 11:30.

say that so it is. And he who hath it not doth not even believe in it; how then can he come to know it?

On the other hand, the life of the natural man, where he hath a lively, subtle, cunning nature, is so manifold and complex, and seeketh and inventeth so many turnings and windings and falsehoods for its own ends, and that so continually, that this also is neither to be uttered nor set forth.

Now, since all falsehood is deceived, and all deception beginneth in self-deception, so is it also with this false Light and Life, for he who deceiveth is also deceived, as we have said before. And in this false Light and Life is found everything that belongeth to the Evil Spirit and is his, insomuch that they cannot be discerned apart; for the false Light is the Evil Spirit, and the Evil Spirit is this false Light. Hereby we may know this. For even as the Evil Spirit thinketh himself to be God, or would fain be God, or be thought to be God, and in all this is so utterly deceived that he doth not think himself to be deceived, so is it also with this false Light, and the Love and Life that is thereof. And as the Devil would fain deceive all men, and draw them to himself and his works, and make them like himself, and useth much art and cunning to this end, so is it also with this false Light; and as no one may turn the Evil Spirit from his own way, so no one can turn this deceived and deceitful Light from its errors. And the cause thereof is, that both these two, the Devil and Nature, vainly think that they are not deceived, and that it standeth quite well with them. And this is the very worst and most mischievous delusion. Thus the Devil and Nature are one, and where nature is conquered the Devil is also conquered, and, in like manner, where nature is not conquered the Devil is not conquered. Whether as touching the outward life in the world, or the inward life of the spirit, this false Light continueth in its state of blindness and falsehood, so that it is both deceived itself and deceiveth others with it, wheresoever it may.

From what hath here been said, ye may understand and perceive more than hath been expressly set forth. For whenever we speak of the

Adam, and disobedience, and of the old man, of self-seeking, self-will, and self-serving, of the I, the Me, and the Mine, nature, falsehood, the Devil, sin; it is all one and the same thing. These are all contrary to God, and remain without God.

44.
How nothing is contrary to God but Self-will and how he who seeketh his own Good for his own sake, findeth it not; and how a Man of himself neither knoweth nor can do any good Thing.

Now, it may be asked; is there aught which is contrary to God and the true Good? I say, No. Likewise, there is nothing without God, except to will otherwise than is willed by the Eternal Will; that is, contrary to the Eternal Will. Now the Eternal Will willeth that nothing be willed or loved but the Eternal Goodness. And where it is otherwise, there is something contrary to Him, and in this sense it is true that he who is without God is contrary to God; but in truth there is no Being contrary to God or the true Good.

We must understand it as though God said: "He who willeth without Me, or willeth not what I will, or otherwise than as I will, he willeth contrary to Me, for My will is that no one should will otherwise than I, and that there should be no will without Me, and without My will; even as without Me, there is neither Substance, nor Life, nor this, nor that, so also there should be no Will apart from Me, and without My will." And even as in truth all beings are one in substance in the Perfect Being, and all good is one in the One Being, and so forth, and cannot exist without that One, so shall all wills be one in the One Perfect Will, and there shall be no will apart from that One. And whatever is otherwise is wrong, and contrary to God and His will, and therefore it is sin. Therefore all will apart from God's will (that is, all self-will) is sin, and so is all that is done from self-will. So long as a man seeketh his own will and his own highest Good, because it is His and for his own sake, he will never find it; for so long as he doeth this, he is not seeking his own highest Good, and how then should he find it? For so long as he doeth this, he seeketh himself, and dreameth that he is himself the highest Good; and seeing that he is not the highest Good, he seeketh not the highest Good, so long as he seeketh himself. But whosoever seeketh, loveth, and pursueth Goodness as Goodness and for the sake of Goodness, and maketh that his end, for nothing but the love of Goodness, not for love of the I, Me, Mine, Self, and the like, he will find the highest Good, for he seeketh it aright, and they who seek it otherwise do err. And truly it is on this wise that the true and Perfect Goodness seeketh and loveth and pursueth itself, and therefore it findeth itself.

It is a great folly when a man, or any creature, dreameth that he knoweth or can accomplish aught of himself, and above all when he dreameth that he knoweth or can fulfil any good thing, whereby he may deserve much at God's hands, and prevail with Him. If he understood rightly, he would see that this is to put a great affront upon God. But the True and Perfect Goodness hath compassion on the foolish simple man who knoweth no better, and ordereth things for the best for him, and giveth him as much of the good things of God as he is able to receive. But as we have said afore, he findeth and receiveth not the True Good so long as he remaineth unchanged; for unless Self and Me depart, he will never find or receive it.

45.
How that where there is a Christian Life, Christ dwelleth, and how Christ's Life is the best and most admirable Life that ever hath been or can be.

He who knoweth and understandeth Christ's life, knoweth and understandeth Christ Himself; and in like manner, he who understandeth not His life, doth not understand Christ Himself. And he who believeth on Christ, believeth that His life is the best and noblest life that can be, and if a man believe not this, neither doth he believe on Christ Himself. And in so far as a man's life is according to Christ, Christ Himself dwelleth in him, and if he hath not the one neither hath he the other. For where there is the life of Christ, there is Christ Himself, and where His life is not, Christ is not, and where a man hath His life, he may say with St. Paul, "I live, yet not I, but Christ liveth in me."[47] And this is the noblest and best life; for in him who hath it, God Himself dwelleth, with all goodness. So how could there be a better life? When we speak of obedience, of the new man, of the True Light, the True Love, or the life of Christ, it is all the same thing, and where one of these is, there are they all, and where one is wanting, there is none of them, for they are all one in truth and substance. And whatever may bring about that new birth which maketh alive in Christ, to that let us cleave with all our might and to nought else; and let us forswear and flee all that may hinder it. And he who hath received this life in the Holy Sacrament, hath verily and indeed received Christ, and the more of that life he hath received, the more he hath received of Christ, and the less, the less of Christ.

---

47 Galatians 2:20.

46.

How entire Satisfaction and true Rest are to be found in God alone, and not in any Creature; and how he who Will be obedient unto God, must also be obedient to the Creatures, with all Quietness, and he who would love God, must love all Things in One.

It is said, that he who is content to find all his satisfaction in God, hath enough; and this is true. And he who findeth satisfaction in aught which is this and that, findeth it not in God; and he who findeth it in God, findeth it in nothing else, but in that which is neither this nor that, but is All. For God is One and must be One, and God is All and must be All. And now what is, and is not One, is not God; and what is, and is not All and above All, is also not God, for God is One and above One, and All and above All. Now he who findeth full satisfaction in God, receiveth all his satisfaction from One source, and from One only, as One. And a man cannot find all satisfaction in God, unless all things are One to him, and One is All, and something and nothing are alike.[48] But where it should be thus, there would be true satisfaction, and not else.

    Therefore also, he who will wholly commit himself unto God and be obedient to Him, must also resign himself to all things, and be willing to suffer them, without resisting or defending himself or calling for succour. And he who doth not thus resign or submit himself to all things in One as One, doth not resign or submit himself to God. Let us look at Christ. And he who shall and will lie still under God's hand, must lie still under all things in One as One, and in no wise withstand any suffer-

---

48 Literally *aught* and *nought, itch und nicht;* but *aught* means *any* thing, the idea of the original is emphatically *some* thing, a part, not the whole.—Tr.

ing. Such an one were a Christ. And he who fighteth against affliction, and refuseth to endure it, is truly fighting against God. That is to say, we may not withstand any creature or thing by force of war, either in will or works. But we may indeed, without sin, prevent affliction, or avoid it, or flee from it.

Now he who shall or will love God, loveth all things in One as All, One and All, and One in All as All in One; and he who loveth somewhat, this or that, otherwise than in the One, and for the sake of the One, loveth not God; for he loveth somewhat which is not God. Therefore he loveth it more than God. Now he who loveth somewhat more than God or along with God, loveth not God, for He must be and will be alone loved, and verily nothing ought to be loved but God alone. And when the true divine Light and Love dwell in a man, he loveth nothing else but God alone, for he loveth God as Goodness and for the sake of Goodness, and all Goodness as One, and one as All; for, in truth, All is One and One is All in God.

47.
A Question: Whether, if we ought to love all Things, we ought to love Sin also?

Some may put a question here and say: "If we are to love all things, must we then love sin too?" I answer: No. When I say "all things," I mean all Good; and all that is, is good, in so far as it hath Being. The Devil is good in so far as he hath Being. In this sense nothing is evil, or not good. But sin is to will, desire, or love otherwise than as God doth. And Willing is not Being, therefore it is not good. Nothing is good except in so far as it is in God and with God. Now all things have their Being in God, and more truly in God than in themselves, and therefore all things are good in so far as they have a Being, and if there were aught that had not its Being in God, it would not be good. Now behold, the willing or desiring which is contrary to God is not in God; for God cannot will or desire anything contrary to Himself, or otherwise than Himself. Therefore it is evil or not good, and is merely nought.

God loveth also works, but not all works. Which then? Such as are done from the teaching and guidance of the True Light and the True Love; and what is done from these and in these, is done in spirit and in truth, and what is thereof, is God's, and pleaseth Him well. But what is done of the false Light and false Love, is all of the Wicked One; and especially what happeneth, is done or left undone, wrought or suffered from any other will, or desire, or love, than God's will, or desire, or love. This is, and cometh to pass, without God and contrary to God, and is utterly contrary to good works, and is altogether sin.

48.
How we must believe certain Things of God's Truth beforehand, ere we can come to a true Knowledge and Experience thereof.

Christ said, "He that believeth not," or will not or cannot believe, "shall be damned." It is so of a truth; for a man, while he is in this present time, hath not knowledge; and he cannot attain unto it, unless he first believe. And he who would know before he believeth, cometh never to true knowledge. We speak not here of the articles of the Christian faith, for every one believeth them, and they are common to every Christian man, whether he be sinful or saved, good or wicked; and they must be believed in the first place, for without that, one cannot come to know them. But we are speaking of a certain Truth which it is possible to know by experience, but which ye must believe in, before that ye know it by experience, else ye will never come to know it truly. This is the faith of which Christ speaketh in that saying of His.

49.
Of Self-will, and how Lucifer and Adam fell away from God through Self-will.

It hath been said, that there is of nothing so much in hell as of self-will. The which is true, for there is nothing else there than self-will, and if there were no self-will, there would be no Devil and no hell. When it is said that Lucifer fell from Heaven, and turned away from God and the like, it meaneth nothing else than that he would have his own will, and would not be at one with the Eternal Will. So was it likewise with Adam in Paradise. And when we say Self-will, we mean, to will otherwise than as the One and Eternal Will of God willeth.

50.
How this present Time is a Paradise and outer Court of Heaven, and how therein there is only one Tree forbidden, that is, Self-will.

What is Paradise? All things that are; for all are goodly and pleasant, and therefore may fitly be called a Paradise. It is said also, that Paradise is an outer court of Heaven. Even so this world is verily an outer court of the Eternal, or of Eternity, and specially whatever in Time, or any temporal things or creatures, manifesteth or remindeth us of God or Eternity; for the creatures are a guide and a path unto God and Eternity. Thus this world is an outer court of Eternity, and therefore it may well be called a Paradise, for it is such in truth. And in this Paradise, all things are lawful, save one tree and the fruits thereof. That is to say: of all things that are, nothing is forbidden and nothing is contrary to God but one thing only: that is, Self-will, or to will otherwise than as the Eternal Will would have it. Remember this. For God saith to Adam, that is, to every man, "Whatever thou art, or doest, or leavest undone, or whatever cometh to pass, is all lawful and not forbidden if it be not done from or according to thy will, but for the sake of and according to My will. But all that is done from thine own Will is contrary to the Eternal Will."

It is not that every work which is thus wrought is in itself contrary to the Eternal Will, but in so far as it is wrought from a different will, or otherwise than from the Eternal and Divine Will.

51.
Wherefore God hath created Self-will, seeing that it is so contrary to Him.

Now some may ask: "Since this tree, to wit, Self-will, is so contrary to God and the Eternal Will, wherefore hath God created it, and set it in Paradise?"

Answer: whatever man or creature desireth to dive into and understand the secret counsel and will of God, so that he would fain know wherefore God doeth this, or doeth not that, and the like, desireth the same as Adam and the Devil. For this desire is seldom from aught else than that the man taketh delight in knowing, and glorieth therein, and this is sheer pride. And so long as this desire lasteth, the truth will never be known, and the man is even as Adam or the Devil. A truly humble and enlightened man doth not desire of God that He should reveal His secrets unto him, and ask wherefore God doeth this or that, or hindereth or alloweth such a thing, and so forth; but he desireth only to know how he may please God, and become as nought in himself, having no will, and that the Eternal Will may live in him, and have full possession of him, undisturbed by any other will, and how its due may be rendered to the Eternal Will, by him and through him.

However, there is yet another answer to this question, for we may say: the most noble and delightful gift that is bestowed on any creature is that of perceiving, or Reason, and Will. And these two are so bound together, that where the one is, there the other is also. And if it were not for these two gifts, there would be no reasonable creatures, but only brutes and brutishness; and that were a great loss, for God would never have His due, and behold Himself and His attributes manifested in deeds and works; the which ought to be, and is, necessary to perfection. Now, behold, Perception and Reason are created and bestowed along with Will, to the intent that they may instruct the will and also themselves, that neither perception nor will is of itself, nor is nor ought to be unto itself, nor ought to seek or obey itself. Neither shall they turn themselves to their own advantage, nor make use of themselves to their own ends and purposes; for His they are from Whom they do proceed, and unto Him shall they submit, and flow back into Him, and become nought in themselves, that is, in their selfishness.

But here ye must consider more particularly, somewhat touching the Will. There is an Eternal Will, which is in God a first Principle and substance, apart from all works and effects,[49] and the same will is in Man, or the creature, willing certain things, and bringing them to pass. For it belongeth unto the Will, and is its property, that it shall will something. What else is it for? For it were in vain, unless it had some work to do, and this it cannot have without the creature. Therefore there must be creatures, and God will have them, to the end that the Will may be put in exercise by their means, and work, which in God is and must be without work. Therefore the will in the creature, which we call a created will, is as truly God's as the Eternal Will, and is not of the creature.

---

49 Or *realisation*, wirklichkeit.

And now, since God cannot bring His will into exercise, working and causing changes, without the creature, therefore it pleaseth Him to do so in and with the creature. Therefore the will is not given to be exerted by the creature, but only by God, who hath a right to work out His own will by means of the will which is in man, and yet is God's. And in whatever man or creature it should be purely and wholly thus, the will would be exerted not by the man but by God, and thus it would not be self-will, and the man would not will otherwise than as God willeth; for God Himself would move the will and not man. And thus the will would be one with the Eternal Will, and flow out into it, though the man would still keep his sense of liking and disliking, pleasure and pain, and the like. For wherever the will is exerted, there must be a sense of liking and disliking; for if things go according to his will, the man liketh it, and if they do not, he disliketh it, and this liking and disliking are not of the man's producing, but of God's. For whatever is the source of the will, is the source of these also.[50] Now the will cometh not of man but of God, therefore liking and disliking come from Him also. But nothing is complained of, save only what is contrary to God. So also there is no joy but of God alone, and that which is His and belongeth unto Him. And as it is with the will, so is it also with perception, reason, gifts, love, and all the powers of man; they are all of God, and not of man. And wherever the will should be altogether surrendered to God, the rest would of a certainty be surrendered likewise, and God would have His right, and the man's will would not be his own. Behold, therefore hath God created the will, but not that it should be self-will.

Now cometh the Devil or Adam, that is to say, false nature, and taketh this will unto itself and maketh the same its own, and useth it for itself and its own ends. And this is the mischief and wrong, and the bite that Adam made in the apple, which is forbidden, because it is contrary to God. And therefore, so long as there is any self-will, there will never be true love, true peace, true rest. This we see both in man and in the

---

50 This sentence is found in Luther's edition, but not in that based on the Wurtzburg Manuscript.

Devil. And there will never be true blessedness either in time or eternity, where this self-will is working, that is to say, where man taketh the will unto himself and maketh it his own. And if it be not surrendered in this present time, but carried over into eternity, it may be foreseen that it will never be surrendered, and then of a truth there will never be content, nor rest, nor blessedness; as we may see by the Devil. If there were no reason or will in the creatures, God were, and must remain for ever, unknown, unloved, unpraised, and unhonoured, and all the creatures would be worth nothing, and were of no avail to God. Behold thus the question which was put to us is answered.[51] And if there were any who, by my much writing (which yet is brief and profitable in God), might be led to amend their ways, this were indeed well-pleasing unto God.

That which is free, none may call his own, and he who maketh it his own, committeth a wrong. Now, in the whole realm of freedom, nothing is so free as the will, and he who maketh it his own, and suffereth it not to remain in its excellent freedom, and free nobility, and in its free exercise, doeth a grievous wrong. This is what is done by the Devil and Adam and all their followers. But he who leaveth the will in its noble freedom doeth right, and this doth Christ with all His followers. And whoso robbeth the will of its noble freedom and maketh it his own, must of necessity as his reward, be laden with cares and troubles, with discontent, disquiet, unrest, and all manner of wretchedness, and this will remain and endure in time and in eternity. But he who leaveth the will in its freedom, hath content, peace, rest, and blessedness in time and in eternity. Wherever there is a man in whom the will is not enslaved, but continueth noble and free, there is a true freeman not in bondage to any, one of those to whom Christ said: "The truth shall make you free"; and immediately after, he saith: "If the Son shall make you free, ye shall be free indeed."[52]

Furthermore, mark ye that where the will enjoyeth its freedom, it

---

51 Namely, why God hath created the will.
52 John 8:32-36.

hath its proper work, that is, willing. And where it chooseth whatever it will unhindered, it always chooseth in all things what is noblest and best, and all that is not noble and good it hateth, and findeth to be a grief and offence unto it. And the more free and unhindered the will is, the more is it pained by evil, injustice, iniquity, and in short all manner of wickedness and sin, and the more do they grieve and afflict it. This we see in Christ, whose will was the purest and the least fettered or brought into bondage of any man's that ever lived. So likewise was Christ's human nature the most free and single of all creatures, and yet felt the deepest grief, pain, and indignation at sin that any creature ever felt. But when men claim freedom for their own, so as to feel no sorrow or indignation at sin and what is contrary to God, but say that we must heed nothing and care for nothing, but be, in this present time, as Christ was after His resurrection, and the like;—this is no true and divine freedom springing from the true divine Light, but a natural, unrighteous, false, and deceitful freedom, springing from a natural, false, and deluded light.

Were there no self-will, there would be also no ownership. In heaven there is no ownership; hence there are found content, true peace, and all blessedness. If any one there took upon him to call anything his own, he would straightway be thrust out into hell, and would become an evil spirit. But in hell everyone will have self-will, therefore there is all manner of misery and wretchedness. So is it also here on earth. But if there were one in hell who should get quit of his self-will and call nothing his own, he would come out of hell into heaven. Now, in this present time, man is set between heaven and hell, and may turn himself towards which he will. For the more he hath of ownership, the more he hath of hell and misery; and the less of self-will, the less of hell, and the nearer he is to the Kingdom of Heaven. And could a man, while on earth, be wholly quit of self-will and ownership, and stand up free and at large in God's true light, and continue therein, he would be sure of the Kingdom of Heaven. He who hath something, or seeketh or longeth to have something of his own, is himself a slave; and he who hath nothing of his own, nor seeketh nor longeth thereafter, is free and at large, and in bondage to none.

All that hath here been said, Christ taught in words and fulfilled in works for three-and-thirty years, and He teacheth it to us very briefly when He saith: "Follow Me." But he who will follow Him must forsake all things, for He renounced all things so utterly as no man else hath ever done. Moreover, he who will come after Him, must take up the cross, and the cross is nothing else than Christ's life, for that is a bitter cross to nature. Therefore He saith: "And he that taketh not his cross, and followeth after Me, is not worthy of Me, and cannot be My disciple."[53] But nature, in her false freedom, weeneth she hath forsaken all things, yet she will have none of the cross, and saith she hath had enough of it already, and needeth it no longer, and thus she is deceived. For had she ever tasted the cross she would never part with it again. He that believeth on Christ must believe all that is here written.

52.
How we must take those two Sayings of Christ: "No Man cometh unto the Father, but by Me," and "No Man cometh unto Me, except the Father which hath sent Me draw him."

Christ saith: "No man cometh unto the Father, but by Me."[54] Now mark how we must come unto the Father through Christ. The man shall set a watch over himself and all that belongeth to him within and without, and shall so direct, govern, and guard his heart, as far as in him lieth, that neither will nor desire, love nor longing, opinion nor thought, shall spring up in his heart, or have any abiding-place in him, save such as are

---

53   Matt. 10:38, and Luke 14:27.
54   John 14:6.

meet for God and would beseem him well, if God Himself were made Man. And whenever he becometh aware of any thought or intent rising up within him that doth not belong to God and were not meet for Him, he must resist it and root it out as thoroughly and as Speedily as he may.

By this rule he must order his outward behaviour, whether he work or refrain, speak or keep silence, wake or sleep, go or stand still. In short: in all his ways and walks, whether as touching his own business, or his dealings with other men, he must keep his heart with all diligence, lest he do aught, or turn aside to aught, or suffer aught to spring up or dwell within him or about him, or lest anything be done in him or through him, otherwise than were meet for God, and would be possible and seemly if God Himself were verily made Man.

Behold! he, in whom it should be thus, whatever he had within, or did without, would be all of God, and the man would be in his life a follower of Christ more truly than we can understand or set forth. And he who led such a life would go in and out through Christ; for he would be a follower of Christ: therefore also he would come with Christ and through Christ unto the Father. And he would be also a servant of Christ, for he who cometh after Him is His servant, as He Himself also saith: "If any man serve Me, let him follow Me; and where I am, there shall also my servant be."[55] And he who is thus a servant and follower of Christ, cometh to that place where Christ Himself is; that is, unto the Father. As Christ Himself saith: "Father, I will that they also, whom Thou hast given Me, be with Me where I am."[56] Behold, he who walketh in this path, "entereth in by the door into the sheepfold," that is, into eternal life; "and to him the porter openeth";[57] but he who entereth in by some other way, or vainly thinketh that he would or can come to the Father or to eternal blessedness otherwise than through Christ, is

---

55 John 12:26.
56 John 17:24.
57 John 10:1, 3.

deceived; for he is not in the right Way, nor entereth in by the right Door. Therefore to him the porter openeth not, for he is a thief and a murderer, as Christ saith.

Now, behold and mark, whether one can be in the right Way, and enter in by the right Door, if one be living in lawless freedom or license, or disregard of ordinances, virtue or vice, order or disorder, and the like. Such liberty we do not find in Christ, neither is it in any of His true followers.

53.
Considereth that other saying of Christ, "No Man can come unto Me, except the Father, which hath sent Me, draw him."

Christ hath also said: "No man cometh unto Me, except the Father, which hath sent Me, draw him."[58] Now mark: by the Father, I understand the Perfect, Simple Good, which is All and above All, and without which and besides which there is no true Substance, nor true Good, and without which no good work ever was or will be done. And in that it is All, it must be in All and above All. And it cannot be any one of those things which the creatures, as creatures, can comprehend or understand. For whatever the creature, as creature (that is, in her creature kind), can conceive of and understand, is something, this or that, and therefore is some sort of creature. And now if the Simple Perfect Good were somewhat, this or that, which the creature understandeth, it would not be the All, nor the Only One, and therefore not Perfect. Therefore also it cannot be named, seeing that it is none of all the things which the creature as creature can comprehend, know, conceive, or name. Now behold, when this Perfect Good, which is unnameable, floweth into a Person

---

58   John 6:44.

able to bring forth, and bringeth forth the Only-begotten Son in that Person, and itself in Him, we call it the Father.

Now mark how the Father draweth men unto Christ. When somewhat of this Perfect Good is discovered and revealed within the soul of man, as it were in a glance or flash, the soul conceiveth a longing to approach unto the Perfect Goodness, and unite herself with the Father. And the stronger this yearning groweth, the more is revealed unto her; and the more is revealed unto her, the more is she drawn toward the Father, and her desire quickened. Thus is the soul drawn and quickened into a union with the Eternal Goodness. And this is the drawing of the Father, and thus the soul is taught of Him who draweth her unto Himself, that she cannot enter into a union with Him except she come unto Him by the life of Christ. Behold, now she putteth on that life of which I have spoken afore.

Now see the meaning of these two sayings of Christ's. The one, "No man cometh unto the Father, but by Me"; that is, through My life, as hath been set forth. The other saying, "No man cometh unto Me, except the Father draw him"; that is, he doth not take My life upon him and come after Me, except he be moved and drawn of My Father; that is, of the Simple and Perfect Good, of which St. Paul saith; "when that which is Perfect is come, then that which is in part shall be done away." That is to say; in whatever soul this Perfect Good is known, felt and tasted, so far as may be in this present time, to that soul all created things are as nought compared with this Perfect One, as in truth they are; for beside or without the Perfect One, is neither true Good nor true Substance. Whosoever then hath, or knoweth, or loveth, the Perfect One, hath and knoweth all goodness. What more then doth he want, or what is all that "is in part" to him, seeing that all the parts are united in the Perfect, in One Substance?

What hath here been said, concerneth the outward life, and is a good way or access unto the true inward life; but the inward life beginneth after this. When a man hath tasted that which is perfect as far as is possible in this present time, all created things and even himself become as nought to him. And when he perceiveth of a truth that the Perfect One is All and above All, he needs must follow after Him, and ascribe all that is good, such as Substance, Life, Knowledge, Reason, Power, and the like, unto Him alone and to no creature. And hence followeth that the man claimeth for his own neither Substance, Life, Knowledge, nor Power, Doing nor Refraining, nor anything that we can call good. And thus the man becometh so poor, that he is nought in himself, and so are also all things unto him which are somewhat, that is, all created things. And then there beginneth in him a true inward life, wherein from henceforward, God Himself dwelleth in the man, so that nothing is left in him but what is God's or of God, and nothing is left which taketh anything unto itself. And thus God Himself, that is, the One Eternal Perfectness, alone is, liveth, knoweth, worketh, loveth, willeth, doeth and refraineth in the man. And thus, of a truth, it should be, and where it is not so, the man hath yet far to travel, and things are not altogether right with him.

Furthermore, it is a good way and access unto this life, to feel always that what is best is dearest, and always to prefer the best, and cleave to it, and unite oneself to it. First: in the creatures. But what is best in the creatures? Be assured: that, in which the Eternal Perfect Goodness and what is thereof, that is, all which belongeth thereunto, most brightly shineth and worketh, and is best known and loved. But what is that which is of God, and belongeth unto Him? I answer: whatever with justice and truth we do, or might call good.

When therefore among the creatures the man cleaveth to that which is the best that he can perceive, and keepeth steadfastly to that, in singleness of heart, he cometh afterward to what is better and better, until, at last, he findeth and tasteth that the Eternal Good is a Perfect Good, without measure and number above all created good. Now if what is best is to be dearest to us, and we are to follow after it, the One Eternal Good must be loved above all and alone, and we must cleave to Him alone, and unite ourselves with Him as closely as we may. And now if we are to ascribe all goodness to the One Eternal Good, as of right and truth we ought, so must we also of right and truth ascribe unto Him the beginning, middle, and end of our course, so that nothing remain to man or the creature. So it should be of a truth, let men say what they will.

Now on this wise we should attain unto a true inward life. And what then further would happen to the soul, or would be revealed unto her, and what her life would be henceforward, none can declare or guess. For it is that which hath never been uttered by man's lips, nor hath it entered into the heart of man to conceive.

In this our long discourse, are briefly comprehended those things which ought of right and truth to be fulfilled: to wit, that man should claim nothing for his own, nor crave, will, love, or intend anything but God alone, and what is like unto Him, that is to say, the One, Eternal, Perfect Goodness.

But if it be not thus with a man, and he take, will, purpose, or crave, somewhat for himself, this or that, whatever it may be, beside or other than the Eternal and Perfect Goodness which is God Himself, this is all too much and a great injury, and hindereth the man from a perfect life; wherefore he can never reach the Perfect Good, unless he first forsake all things and himself first of all. For no man can serve two masters, who are contrary the one to the other; he who will have the one, must let the other go. Therefore if the Creator shall enter in, the creature must depart. Of this be assured.

54.
How a Man shall not seek his own, either in Things spiritual or natural but the Honour of God only; and how he must enter in by the right Door, to wit, by Christ, into Eternal Life.

If a man may attain thereunto, to be unto God as his hand is to a man, let him be therewith content, and not seek farther. This is my faithful counsel, and here I take my stand. That is to say, let him strive and wrestle with all his might to obey God and His commandments so thoroughly at all times and in all things, that in him there be nothing, spiritual or natural, which opposeth God; and that his whole soul and body with all their members may stand ready and willing for that to which God hath created them; as ready and willing as his hand is to a man, which is so wholly in his power, that in the twinkling of an eye, he moveth and turneth it whither he will. And when we find it otherwise with us, we must give our whole diligence to amend our state; and this from love and not from fear, and in all things whatsoever, seek and intend the glory and praise of God alone. We must not seek our own, either in things spiritual or in things natural. It must needs be thus, if it is to stand well with us. And every creature oweth this of right and truth unto God, and especially man, to whom, by the ordinance of God, all creatures are made subject, and are servants, that he may be subject to and serve God only.

Further, when a man hath come so far, and climbed so high, that he thinketh and weeneth he standeth sure, let him beware lest the Devil strew ashes and his own bad seed on his heart, and nature seek and take her own comfort, rest, peace, and delight in the prosperity of his soul, and he fall into a foolish, lawless freedom and licentiousness, which is altogether alien to, and at war with, a true life in God. And this will happen to that man who hath not entered, or refuseth to enter in by the right Way and the right Door (which is Christ, as we have said), and imagineth that he would or could come by any other way to the highest truth. He may perhaps dream that he hath attained thereunto, but verily he is in error.

And our witness is Christ, who declareth: "Verily, verily, I say unto you, He that entereth not by the door into the sheepfold, but climbeth up some other way, the same is a thief and a robber."[59] A thief, for he robbeth God of His honour and glory, which belong to God alone; he taketh them unto himself, and seeketh and purposeth himself. A murderer, for he slayeth his own soul, and taketh away her life, which is God. For as the body liveth by the soul, even so the soul liveth by God. Moreover, he murdereth all those who follow him, by his doctrine and example. For Christ saith: "I came down from heaven, not to do Mine own will, but the will of Him that sent Me."[60] And again: "Why call ye Me Lord, Lord?"[61] as if he would say, it will avail you nothing to Eternal life. And again: "Not every one that saith unto Me Lord, Lord, shall enter into the Kingdom of Heaven; but he that doeth the will of My Father which is in Heaven."[62] But He saith also: "If thou wilt enter into life, keep the commandments."[63] And what are the commandments? "To love the Lord thy God with all thy heart, with all thy soul, and with all thy strength, and with all thy mind; and to love thy neighbour as thyself."[64] And in these two commandments all others are briefly comprehended.

There is nothing more precious to God, or more profitable to man, than humble obedience. In His eyes, one good work, wrought from true obedience, is of more value than a hundred thousand, wrought from self-will, contrary to obedience. Therefore he who hath this obedience

---

59 John 10:1.
60 John 6:38.
61 Luke 6:46.
62 Matt. 7:21.
63 Matt. 19:17.
64 Luke 10:27.

need not dread Him, for such a man is in the right way, and following after Christ.

That we may thus deny ourselves, and forsake and renounce all things for God's sake, and give up our own wills, and die unto ourselves, and live unto God alone and to His will, may He help us, who gave up His will to His Heavenly Father,—Jesus Christ our Lord, to whom be blessing for ever and ever. Amen.

THE END

INDEX OF SCRIPTURE REFERENCES

Psalms: 8:2 14:6 49 49:8

Isaiah: 14:13 14:14 42:8 57:21

Matthew: 5:20 7:21 10:20 10:22 10:38 10:38 11:29 11:30 12:30 16:24 19:17 20:28 26:32

Mark: 8:35

Luke: 6:46 10:27 14:26 14:27 24:39

John: 3:3 3:8 3:8 6:38 6:44 8:32-36 10:1 10:1 10:3 12:26 14:6 14:27 15:5 15:15 16:33 17:24

Romans: 6:14 8:14 8:14

1 Corinthians: 4:7 13:10 13:10 15:22

2 Corinthians: 3:5

Galatians: 2:20 4:4

Ephesians: 4:22 4:24

2 Peter: 1:4

Wisdom of Solomon: 10:21

Lightning Source UK Ltd.
Milton Keynes UK
UKOW051242020512

191867UK00001B/266/P